Read This First

Congratulations on grabbing your copy of *Sell More with Webinars!* We are thrilled to have you join our community of smart, driven individuals who are ready to take their sales to the next level using webinars. This book is packed with actionable strategies to help you generate leads, engage your audience, and close more deals. We know that implementing these tactics can be a game-changer for your business, and we're here to support you every step of the way.

As a special thank you for investing in our book, we've put together a collection of supplemental resources designed to help you get results even faster. These bonus materials include exclusive checklists, training videos, & more that will guide you through each stage of the webinar process. To access these free resources, simply scan the QR code or click the link below. Let's get started on supercharging your sales with webinars!

Scan the QR Code here:

or go to https://getwebinarkit.com/book-resources

Sell More With Webinars

The Ultimate Playbook for Exploding Your Business and Automating Your Marketing Success

Stefan Ciancio & Philip Schaffer

www.GameChangerPublishing.com

Foreword

by Anik Singal

How I got involved with webinars is actually a funny story. It all started by accident. I was simply doing a live training on GoToWebinar with a group of low-ticket customers who had bought a personal development product. We began discussing wealth and how I made mine, and I started teaching them how I used to do email marketing, promoting products as an email affiliate.

People were really getting excited about it, and a bunch of them started saying, "We'd like that training, we'd like that training."

On the spot, I said, "All right, guys, I'll tell you what—I'll do a special training. Here's my PayPal."

I don't remember exactly how much I charged—maybe $300 or $500—but I told them that if they sent the money via PayPal, I'd do a special class. I remember getting about 20% of the people on the webinar to pay. It wasn't a huge group—maybe 100 to 150 people—but still, quite a few sent money. I was like, *Whoa, what the heck just happened?* It's not like I was unfamiliar with webinars, but at that time, I didn't think people were doing sales webinars. For me, it was like a light bulb went off, and I realized that this was the first time I got involved with webinars, totally by accident. I was originally just using it for customer fulfillment, but the customers started demanding more, so I made an offer on the spot without even having an order page. I just gave them a PayPal address.

After that, I decided to make things a bit more official. I remember launching a product in the personal development space called "Future of Wealth." It was the second iteration, and this time, I decided to make a whole event out of it. I said, "I'm going to put everyone in a webinar and talk about how I made my wealth." My big turning point came when I took that little test and turned it into a full campaign. But I still did the webinar behind a customer base.

I launched a low-ticket product and then did the webinar for those buyers, which was a game changer for me. Webinars have since become my number one profit-generation tool. I've made 52,000 sales of products priced at $1,000 or more through webinars, mostly by driving traffic from paid ads straight to webinars. The bottom line is that webinars are where I break into profit. They've transformed my business because they've allowed me to get high-quality customers in a scalable format, whether from cold or warm audiences. They work for both. Email Startup Incubator, which started as Inbox Blueprint, has done over $30 million in sales. It's been running since 2015, so it's been nearly ten years.

So, what are the biggest lessons I've learned about webinars over the years?

1. **You've got to learn how to deliver a webinar.** That's super important.
2. **You need a killer offer.** You could do the best webinar in the world, but if your offer isn't amazing, it won't work.
3. **You've got to sell hard.** You don't want to be unethical or disrespectful, but you need to pitch. People often give up too soon. I'll stay on a webinar and pitch for two hours if I have to.

4. **Give people an opportunity to consume your webinar.** Extend the funnel.
5. **There's a specific psychological formula.** You have to guide people through it for a successful webinar. You cannot teach too much—over-teaching is the worst thing you can do. People want just a taste, not the whole meal.

When paid traffic costs started going up a lot in 2019 and 2020, we couldn't make paid traffic to webinars work until we discovered the art of extending the funnel. We spent a lot of time on automation, segmentation, and refining our funnels. That, along with having a killer offer, was when we really unlocked success. I know it sounds counterintuitive, but you can have a subpar webinar with a sexy, amazing offer and still do fine.

You need to have powerful "aha" moments in your webinar—three to five moments that make someone think, *Holy crap! Wow, how did I not think of that?* These could be contrarian methods (where you say the opposite of what's expected and prove it), scientific concepts, or connections that the audience has never made before. From there, have an amazing offer, a golden goose bonus, and a guarantee that removes the risk.

Personally, I think webinars are going to become even more powerful as a backend vehicle in the future. I believe that everyone will use webinars to acquire customers. We're already seeing this in SaaS companies, many of which use automated webinars to onboard customers. I think this trend will extend to e-commerce, supplement companies, digital marketing, coaches, and consultants. Many companies will use webinars as a tool to onboard and indoctrinate their customers, and they'll increase sales through them.

The trends emerging are also exciting—personalization, segmentation, automation, and creating a personalized experience.

I once did a very casual webinar, just wanting to hang out with people, and I ended up making a ton of money. I can't remember exactly how much, but it was enough to make someone say, "What just happened?"

Put simply, webinars can transform a business. They're very important, period. If you want to do direct marketing, this is something you need to learn. This book should instill in you a strong desire to do webinars. You won't be very good at it when you first start, and no book, course, or software can fix that. Only time will get you there. I just hope you start. I hope you do something—that would be a win.

SELL MORE WITH WEBINARS

Sell More With Webinars

The Ultimate Playbook for Exploding Your Business and Automating Your Marketing Success

Stefan Ciancio and Philip Schaffer

©2024 All Rights Reserved. No portion of this book may be reproduced, stored in a retrieval system, or transmitted in any form or by any means—electronic, mechanical, photocopy, recording, scanning, or other—except for brief quotations in critical reviews or articles without the prior permission of the author.

Published by Game Changer Publishing

Paperback ISBN: 978-1-965653-24-1
Hardcover ISBN: 978-1-965653-25-8
Digital ISBN: 978-1-965653-26-5

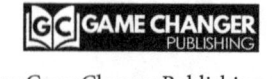

www.GameChangerPublishing.com

Table of Contents

	Introduction	1
Chapter 1	Why Every Business Needs a Webinar, and Why Having One Is Not That Hard	13
Chapter 2	The Four-Step Webinar Framework That Turns Cold Leads Into Hungry Buyers	29
Chapter 3	How to Get Content for Your Webinar in Minutes Even if You Don't Know Where to Start	39
Chapter 4	How to Launch Your Webinar in Record Time Without Technical Skills	45
Chapter 5	How to Present Your Webinar for Maximum Sales Without Stage Fright	57
Chapter 6	How Your Webinar Can Generate Sales Repeatedly Without Needing to Go On Live	63
Chapter 7	How to Use Organic and Paid Marketing Strategies to Drive Targeted Traffic to Your Webinars Every Day	79
Chapter 8	The Little-Known Webinar Formats That Can Increase Your Profit Potential Over 5x	91
Chapter 9	Simple Webinar Extensions You Can Quickly Make to Unlock Long-Term Profits and Beat Your Competitors	105
	Conclusion	119

Introduction

We live in interesting times. Never before in all of history has it been possible to use the internet to reach hundreds of people at a time, deliver the same sales presentation to them, and then be able to sell to multiple people simultaneously. If this had been possible even 40 years ago, every car salesman, real estate agent, knife salesman, and every other type of salesperson in the world would have been foaming at the mouth to get a piece of what is possible today. Yet, so many people still don't take advantage of what's available to them with the invention of the internet. That's what we're hoping to introduce you to in this book: the power of webinars—something so powerful that it can single-handedly transform your business and impact what you're looking for in your life.

Who is this book for? Well, if you're any type of business owner or someone who sells something, you're going to benefit from this book. Whether you have an online business, do coaching, consulting, sell courses, run software, or are a real estate agent or some sort of professional like a chiropractor or a doctor with a product or service you want to get in front of more people—this book is for you. Whatever it is, if you can explain to your audience why it's a great product or service and connect with them, then you have something that's worthy of a webinar.

Through this book, you'll see just how important webinars are in this day and age. Considering how easy it can be for people to actually grow their businesses, and with the technology available to sell things, why are some people crushing it while others struggle so much to sell the very same products? The difference is in the execution, and that's what we're hoping to deliver for you in this book.

Maybe you're struggling to get more leads in your business or make more sales. Maybe you're already making sales but want to figure out how to make more, or perhaps you're just looking to get that first sale and don't have any clue where to start. Maybe you're still working a nine-to-five, and you want to get out of it, and this is just a pipe dream. Maybe you're already selling a decent amount of what you want to sell, but you want to sell more of it. Whatever the case, this is the playbook for you to see what it takes to really take things to the next level.

Before we go any further and talk about webinars, there are a few important things I want you to understand that I've learned on my own business journey. These are precursors to what we're going to be sharing with you in this book. At the end of the day, what we share in this book is what has worked for us for close to a decade now. We've honed our skills, spending countless hours every day learning what works through self-study, attending events and actual field practice, and running well over hundreds, maybe even a thousand webinars, both live and automated.

So, we know a thing or two about what's worked for us in growing various types of businesses—from coaching to many other areas. I'll go into our stories in a minute. But before that, I want to share a few pieces of advice.

If you follow what we teach you here in this book, you're going to be applying what actually works. This isn't a theory taught by some professor in a school who has never actually been in the real world. This is taught by people who have done this for nearly a decade. So, you're literally learning from people who know what works. If you apply what's in this book, it could be a secret weapon you can use to sell just about anything. As I said earlier, you can use this to sell everything from physical products to digital products to programs. Whatever it is, if you can learn this skill—and I promise you it's not that hard to learn, especially with the way we've laid it out for you in this book—you'll have the secret weapon to take your business to the next level.

Now, on that note, I want to share something extremely powerful that I've learned over the last five to ten years. That lesson is to be very careful about who you take advice from. At the end of the day, I want you to look at the person giving you advice about your business and your life. The first question you should ask yourself is, *Does this person have the life or the business that I actually want?* If the answer is no, I highly advise you to take their opinions with a grain of salt. I'm not saying to fully discount them, but you need to understand that this person has not achieved what you want to achieve.

So, be very careful about listening to them regarding whether what you want to achieve is possible or how to go about it. It's better to listen to people who have actually achieved what you want to achieve. In my business career, much of my success has come from modeling what has already worked. Once I stopped listening to the naysayers—the people who told me what I was doing was stupid or wouldn't work—and started connecting with those who believed in what I was doing and believed in me, everything changed for me. So, in addition to having the right strategy, I urge you to try to surround yourself with the right narrative and people because it will make all the difference.

With that being said, I want to congratulate you on making it this far. At the end of the day, you've taken the first step towards building your own success, which is being open-minded and willing to learn new things from people who have actually achieved what you want to achieve. We hope you enjoy the knowledge we're going to share in this book.

Now, let me share why we wrote this book, which ties into what I just said. We wanted to give you a roadmap and the confidence you need to learn the current skill of what's working now to sell more of whatever it is you want to sell. By doing that, you're obviously working toward your bigger picture, whatever your bigger goal is beyond just growing your business. Maybe it's spending more time with your family, achieving total financial freedom to travel the world, or generating a side income. Whatever it is, this book will be your North Star, guiding you on what you need to do to take things to the next level.

So, with this out of the way, what is this magical piece that's going to allow you to do that? The magical piece we've alluded to is webinars. Before we get started, we want to cover how anyone can run a webinar. One of the main points we want to make clear as you read this book is that anyone can build and run a webinar and see great results with it. You might think it's an agonizing process that will take a ton of time, hard work, blood, sweat, and tears. But as you'll see as you go through this book, creating and running a webinar that benefits you and your business is more attainable than ever before. But before we dive any further into that, let's talk a little bit more about us, the authors, and why you should listen to us.

Stefan's Story

When I first started in online business, my goal was to get out of my engineering nine-to-five job in Connecticut. I was unfulfilled, felt like I was wasting away, and was living in a place with no one my age. I felt like the soil was dry, and there was no garden in which I was going to grow and thrive. At the time, the co-author of this book, Phil, a good friend of mine, was living in New York City and working a software engineering job. I wanted to figure out how to get from point A—boring Connecticut, where I was withering away at a job I hated—to point B, living in an awesome city, growing a company I actually wanted, and being able to travel the world. I'm happy to say I've achieved that dream, and a big part of that was due to webinars.

Along the journey, I started with blogs, niche blogs, and SEO websites, where I would drive traffic and try to make money from the sites. Additionally, I discovered there was a lot of money in selling courses. I said to myself, *If I can figure out how to sell a course and make money passively, I could get out of my job and live the life I actually want.* However, it was a journey learning how to sell courses. A big part of it was affiliate marketing.

I connected with people worldwide who also wanted to build and sell courses. Some were ahead of others, some were just starting out, and I learned how to sell courses. When I started, I sold my courses for incredibly low prices. For this, a sales page was just fine. However, as I wanted to raise my course prices from tens of dollars to hundreds and, in some cases, even thousands of dollars, I noticed something was missing. I needed something that would build enough trust for someone over the internet to trust me with hundreds or even thousands of dollars at a time, and that wasn't going to be a sales page. That's when I discovered the power of webinars. I saw them being used to sell various things online, and I loved them for many reasons, which we'll discuss in this book. One reason is that you can sell to many people at once.

Another reason is that they build a high level of trust because you're building an actual relationship with people. We'll talk more about that in this book, but that's a huge part of how I transitioned from selling things for very cheap to charging much more for my products and services. To this day, I've used webinars to sell almost everything.

I was able to leave my job in September 2015. Since then, I've lived in New York City and Philadelphia and spent a good part of two years traveling the world. Over the last ten years, I've been to 20 countries with no plans of slowing down. All of this is possible due to the power of webinars. My business has taken many iterations over this time, and I've sold coaching, consulting, courses, and SaaS programs—all with the power of webinars. As we've talked about, we're condensing all the information we've learned that works right here into this book. With that said, let's hear Phil's story.

Phil's Story

I originally started my professional career in the corporate world, building software for a Fortune 500 company. But I always had an entrepreneurial streak. Before entering the corporate workforce while I was in college, I built and sold apps and games for mobile phones in the "early days" of the smartphone revolution.

After graduating, I even briefly considered forgoing a "real job" altogether and giving full-time self-employment a shot before being talked out of it by my friends. Despite being talked out of that idea and into getting a "real job" in the corporate world, I still couldn't shake the entrepreneurial bug. As my fresh-faced, out-of-school optimism rapidly faded in the corporate world, and it dawned on me that I might have to work a nine-to-five job for the rest of my life, I turned back to entrepreneurial ventures on the side. I saw some limited success but also faced a lot of failure in those early days.

But after years of toiling away at side hustles while progressively becoming more and more disillusioned with the corporate world, I finally managed to turn a side hustle into something that could make a full-time income. I built up my savings and decided to take the plunge, going all-in on entrepreneurship. It took a few years and most of my savings before I found my footing as an entrepreneur, eventually finding my way back to building and selling software. That's where webinars truly entered my life and changed it for the better.

After building my first subscription software company, I was looking for effective ways to get more customers and subscribers to my app. I tried all sorts of things, but one major breakthrough that made a big difference to the bottom line was a single webinar I created for it. The impact was incredible.

Once I saw the power of webinars, I knew they would be an integral part of any business I had a hand in going forward.

But there was one problem. Even though I saw the power of webinars, there was a major roadblock. At the time, webinar software was clunky, buggy, and very expensive. Being a software engineer, I saw the problem clearly and also saw a potential solution. I consulted with Stefan, my longtime friend, who I'd already worked with on and off over the years. He was already using webinars successfully in his business but encountered the same issues I did with clunky, buggy, and expensive platforms. We both loved webinars but agreed the market was in desperate need of a better solution. So, we decided to partner together to solve the problem for ourselves and others, which is how our webinar platform, WebinarKit, was born.

I immediately dropped everything, including my other growing software business at the time, because I was so enthralled with the webinar opportunity I saw before us. I started working day and night to build the first version of what would become WebinarKit. Building WebinarKit allowed me to gain a deep understanding of all the various pieces that go into building and running a successful webinar, for which I'll always be grateful. Within a few months, the first version of WebinarKit was ready. With Stefan's marketing expertise, we successfully launched our new business to the public, bringing an intuitive, easy-to-use, and inexpensive webinar platform to the market that was desperately needed. The rest is history. Today, we continue to work actively on WebinarKit and use webinars to grow our own businesses, both with WebinarKit and beyond.

As you can probably see by now, webinars are deeply important to both of us and have had a huge impact on our lives. But it's not just us benefiting from the power of webinars. We've continually advocated webinars with our clients, partners, and friends.

For example, a colleague of ours, Trevor, hired us to help him create a program to help people grow their businesses with webinars alongside our software because many people were saying, "Hey, it's great that you're giving us the tool to succeed, but we'd also like some consulting as well as a roadmap."

At one point, we launched a marketing service. One of our clients was a colleague who had a small audience on Instagram, a small email list, and a small Facebook group, helping people travel for free with credit card hacking. I immediately knew this person was sitting on an absolute goldmine. They hired us for our service, and within about two months, we helped them launch their webinar. (It's even easier to do this now, as we'll show you throughout the book. It doesn't need to take anywhere near two months.)

Once his webinar was done, he launched it to his audience, and it was like an atomic bomb went off.

Trevor was able to get 20 new high-ticket clients from the live webinar. He had to create a waitlist because he had so much business coming in that he couldn't keep up with the demand. People were inquiring even days and weeks after the webinar about signing up for his service. He said it was a complete game-changer. He no longer felt stuck at $5K to $10K per month, where he had been for a long time.

He now had the cash flow to hire additional help and a marketing strategy he could turn on and off whenever he liked to get more clients. Isn't that the power we all want in our businesses? The power to turn on and off a special strategy that will bring in new business whenever you want it. This is the skill that separates those who succeed in business from those who don't, and that's exactly the skill we'll be teaching in this book. So, pay close attention because we're breaking it down in a way that's so simple to apply that anyone can do it.

On that note, I want to share one more story about how webinars have impacted my life. You might be thinking, *What if someone knows what a webinar is? Is this some sort of gimmick?* It's not a gimmick.

It's actually the most authentic way to market because, at the end of the day, even people who know what a webinar is will respond to it. I'm the perfect example. For years, I've dealt with back issues. My lower back had two extruded discs, and there was a period where I wasn't even able to sit down properly for about six months. Despite seeing tons of different doctors over the years, I still really struggled at one point. So, I did a Google search in my local area for someone who could help with my particular issues. I found a few different businesses. All were chiropractors with Google reviews around the same level. They all had relatively cookie-cutter websites, making it impossible to differentiate one from the other, except for one having maybe a 4.6-star Google review versus a 4.5-star. Then, I came across one chiropractor who stood out above the rest, and I ended up giving them my business. Why did I choose that chiropractor over all the others?

Well, when I landed on their website, there was one thing different that all the other chiropractors did not have: a webinar presentation. Even though I knew what a webinar was and could follow the marketing formula behind it to a T, I still chose this doctor. Why? Because the content of the webinar demonstrated that he understood my back pain so deeply, I thought, *If what he's saying is true and he can actually relate to my experience, then he must be the guy who can solve my problem*—even though I knew I was following a marketing format. The words he spoke in the presentation convinced me that he understood my pain in a way that none of the other cookie-cutter chiropractic businesses did. This just proves that webinars work in almost any business because they're an authentic way of marketing and delivering your message in a format people can understand, building that trust, and establishing the know, like, and relatability factors. So that chiropractor got my business, and it turns out he's the busiest chiropractor in that area. This is another example of how a webinar can help you stand out, turn it on or off as much as you want to get more clients and become a powerful asset to your business.

So, why do you want to run webinars? You might be saying to yourself, *I want to get more business, I want to get more sales,* right? But we know there's a deeper why behind this. For example, my why, Stefan's why, was that I wanted to have total financial and location freedom in my life. I didn't want to have to go to my boss to get two weeks off a year, which is such a low amount when you think about it. I wanted to be able to travel when and where I wanted, knowing that the income coming in was equal to or greater than that of my old day job without having to deal with a boss who would tell me when I could take time off. That wasn't something I wanted to do for the rest of my life. I wanted freedom. Some people want to keep their jobs and just make more money on the side, and that's totally fine, too.

Whatever you're looking for, whatever your reason is, it's extremely important for you to sit down and think about what that deeper thing is that you're trying to achieve in your life and how selling more with webinars will help you achieve it.

Take a moment and write it down. Remember this as you go through the book because this is your true motivation, and it will help you get the most out of this and apply it to change your business. What we're sharing with you in this book has taken us 10-plus years of marketing experience to learn, and we've done our best to condense the parts you can take from this book and apply them like a secret weapon over and over again to generate more business. As we said, there's never been a time like this in history. This is the time to act and take full advantage of this digital gold rush.

From here, what will we actually be covering in this book? We're going to give you everything you need to succeed with webinars. We'll explain how webinars have changed over time and why it's easier than ever now to build your webinar, market with your webinar, and deliver more sales with the power of Artificial Intelligence (AI) and automation. We're also going to give you a deep understanding of why webinars work so well, rooted in human psychology, and why they will continue to work well for as long as humans exist. We'll be covering these topics in depth throughout the book.

Before we move on to the next chapter, I want to thank you again for taking the time to read this. It means you are truly working on separating yourself from the group of people who don't succeed in business and joining the group who does. Write down why you're doing this because it will give you additional motivation. Think about what goal you have after reading this book. Ideally, it should be to have your very first webinar set up and start using it to drive weekly or even daily sales in your business. We're excited to dive in.

CHAPTER 1

Why Every Business Needs a Webinar, and Why Having One Is Not That Hard

Why Webinars?

Webinars absolutely transformed my business from the very beginning when I was selling low-ticket courses using sales pages. I realized I could charge a lot more for my knowledge, but when I started doing that, I quickly understood that a sales page alone wasn't going to cut it. I needed something deeper, something that built a higher level of trust. That's when I discovered webinars. Webinars allow you to build massive trust, likability, and credibility with your audience, leading to higher-priced sales.

For example, a sales page might build enough trust to get someone to buy a $37 information product. However, it might not be enough for someone to purchase a $997 course, a $5,000 coaching or consulting program, or a $5,000 to $10,000 per month service in marketing or almost any other niche. A webinar, on the other hand, allows you to do just that. Through my own experience and after seeing it work for so many others, including colleagues, clients, and more, I know that webinars have proven to be an essential tool for selling more of the products you want to sell, and they work for virtually any business. The bottom line is that humans buy from humans. When someone knows, likes, and trusts you, they are more likely to buy from you. That's why in-person sales work so well—it's the highest form of trust-building.

Webinars are the closest thing to emulating that experience. They allow you to achieve the human-to-human trust factor without needing to be physically present. On top of that, there are many other benefits to webinars. For one, you don't have to be an expert to be really good at webinars. Anyone can get started with webinars and see results.

If you're thinking that you need to be some sort of expert to get amazing results with webinars, absolutely not. All you need to be is a human being who can connect with another human being. If you can do that, you are qualified to run webinars that could lead to sales beyond your wildest imagination. Webinars have been responsible for my business growth, my colleagues' and clients' businesses, more lead flow, more sales, easier sales, and higher phone close rates if you're selling on the phone. Anyone who has gone through a webinar will have a much higher close rate than someone who hasn't been pre-sold via a webinar.

Additionally, webinars are an extremely effective lead magnet for building your audience. People who sign up for a webinar are typically interested in learning, making them great long-term subscribers to your newsletter. It also results in higher quality buyers; anyone who watches your webinar is likely to become a fan and fully understand your message, meaning they may stick with you for months or even years and continue buying from you. On the other hand, someone who hasn't watched your webinar likely won't understand you as deeply. Watching your webinar is like establishing a relationship, and it's really cool to think of it like a movie.

Movies follow something called the "hero's journey," a script that has been used since the dawn of cinema. They introduce a character, take you on their journey, and get you to relate to them. When you relate to the character, you know them, you like them, you trust them, and you want them to succeed. A webinar functions similarly. Think of it as your own movie. It's a powerful tool for all these reasons.

Remember, you're just building a relationship with many people at once. This is what we call one-to-many selling. When you have to get on a phone call or deliver the same sales presentation repeatedly, it can become incredibly tedious. By the tenth time, you might find yourself thinking, *I can't believe I have to keep doing this for the rest of my life.* But with a webinar, you can literally reduce the number of times you need to give that presentation by orders of magnitude. And with what we'll teach you in this book, you'll also be able to automate the presentation entirely. More on that later. Essentially, you can reduce the time spent delivering the presentation one-on-one and instead build massive relationships with many people simultaneously. This is incredibly powerful.

We've touched on why webinars work so well, but to sum it up, they allow for one-to-many selling, creating a vehicle that gets people to know, like, and trust you for the long term. Just as we can all name a few movie characters we've built emotional bonds with, the same principle applies here. If you can understand this analogy, you'll grasp marketing on a much deeper level and unlock higher potential in your business. The beauty of webinars is that even a mediocre presentation can still succeed. You can be a below-average presenter and still achieve great results. The more you do, the better you'll get. You can automate and scale with webinars to make more while working less. You can use webinars to sell just about anything, and you're at an advantage simply by having a webinar, especially since a lot of your competition might not even know what a webinar is. But luckily, you're reading this book, and we're going to teach you amazing things and give you resources to stay ahead of the game.

Can Anyone Do This?

A common question or concern people have about webinars is, *Can I do this? Isn't it too much work? Don't I need some secret formula to do this?* This is something many people get hung up on when starting out, but quite early on, you'll come to the conclusion that if those people over there running webinars and succeeding with them can do it, so can you. A big point we want to get across as you read this is that you, and anyone who puts their mind to it, can successfully do it, too. You can create and run webinars that dramatically improve your business and, ultimately, your life. There are no special or secret skills required that prevent you from doing this. You don't need to be a public speaking expert. You don't need to come up with some groundbreaking, novel presentation that will blow people away. In fact, a little bit of imperfection during your webinar can make your presentation seem more authentic, helping you connect with your audience and ultimately boosting conversions. And now, it's easier than ever to get started with the right webinar platform with everything you need to build and run your webinars, including the tools to present your webinar to an audience, plus extensive tutorials and help for anything you might need.

With the latest advancements in AI, you no longer need to spend ages creating your slide deck and presentation, which could have been a very time-consuming process in the past. Now, it's easier than ever to get your content ready for your audience in record time. All you need to do is show up, present your materials, and be authentic. So, in summary, for this section, webinars are accessible to everyone, regardless of their technical expertise or just expertise in general.

Platforms like WebinarKit offer user-friendly interfaces that make setup and execution super straightforward. A good webinar platform will provide extensive tutorials, customer support, and templates that guide users through creating and hosting their events. You don't need to be a tech wizard or a seasoned public speaker to host a successful webinar. You can do this.

Having a Webinar Is Now Easier Than Ever

As mentioned earlier, with the latest advancements in technology, building and running your webinar is easier than ever. We want to spend a little more time explaining that to drive the point home. We have a whole chapter focused on automation later, but part of the beauty of webinars is that you can largely automate 95% of the process, so people are signing up and viewing your presentation on autopilot. You can imagine how powerful this is, as it allows you to deliver your message, deeply connect with your audience, and sell 24/7 rather than on a one-on-one basis during sales calls, which can be time-consuming and inefficient. It's much more effective than just selling via a plain old web page or sales page, where many people might bounce off without getting your full message.

As long as you choose the right modern webinar platform built on the latest technology (more on that later), you'll ensure that you're using a non-clunky, non-buggy platform that meets all your needs. This allows you to run automated and live webinars, maximize audience engagement, and get things up and running as fast as possible. Another massive development has been advancements in AI. In the past, one of the biggest bottlenecks people faced when developing their webinars was creating the slide deck and presentation content. This task could be time-consuming and mentally demanding, potentially taking weeks or even months to hone in on your message and content. But now, with AI, it's easier than ever to create your presentation outline and the actual content in comparatively no time. For example, you could use a service like ChatGPT or Cloud AI to generate an outline for your webinar based on just a simple idea or a sentence or two. From there, you can tweak that outline as needed and then leverage AI again to generate the content for each section of your outline or slide deck. Now, you've essentially got a script you can read from or refer to for your entire webinar presentation, and creating it with AI took just minutes instead of days, weeks, or even months. That's how AI is changing the webinar game and making this more attainable than ever. But most people still don't know about this, so they're not leveraging it in their businesses and lives. You can take advantage of this knowledge now.

Lastly, with the latest advances in cloud tech, you don't even need to download any clunky apps. Importantly, neither do your registrants and attendees. Those apps often need to be updated every few weeks or months, which is super inconvenient.

Have you ever needed to attend an important meeting or webinar only to find out you have to download an app and create an account to join? Even more annoyingly, you might have already downloaded the app, but it requires an update before you can actually join the meeting or webinar. I've experienced this several times, and there are only a few things that annoy me more. I just want to get on the call, see the presentation content, and speak with who I need to, not spend minutes downloading, updating, and potentially troubleshooting some outdated software. But thanks to the latest advances in technology, you no longer need to worry about that if you're using the right tool. A simple web browser is all you and your attendees need, but more on that later.

You might think these technological advances come with eye-watering prices that will break the bank, but the truth is it's more cost-effective than ever, and with the right software, you can even make money from your webinar platform. More on that later.

The Power of Having the Right Formula

At the end of the day, what's really cool about webinars is that simply getting on a webinar and connecting with people can lead to sales, as you'll hear through various anecdotes in earlier and later parts of this book. However, when you put things in the right order, you can optimize your conversions and maximize the number of people who are going to buy now.

With webinars, we produce two types of buyers. First, there are the "right now" buyers: people who finish your 45-minute to hour-long presentation and go from stranger to sale. You've taken them on a 45-minute journey (or however long your webinar is), and by the end, they are ready to hand over their credit card and make a purchase from you. That's a wild amount of trust to build in such a short time. What's cool is that with the right formula, you can maximize the number of people who purchase now. The second type of buyer is the "later" buyer: the people who really loved your presentation and want to follow you. They'll join your audience, open your emails, follow your future webinars, buy your future products, and help you build a long-term sales ecosystem.

That's the power of having the right formula for webinars. Once you understand this formula, you can apply it to sell virtually anything. You can sell digital products, services, physical products—pretty much anything under the sun—by simply understanding this easy-to-grasp formula.

On the topic of the right formula for webinars, one of my business colleagues was running a dating service. He messaged me one day to let me know that he was thinking of starting a matchmaking service for his dating audience. However, he also told me that he had decided not to do it. I asked him why, and he explained that he had sent an email to his list saying, "Hey, I'm looking to charge thousands of dollars for a matchmaking service. Are you interested?" He said that the overwhelming number of people responded with a no, so he believed this was not something he should pursue.

I laughed a bit and then slapped my forehead. I told him, "You need to understand that you actually need to convert someone. Let's say you're a guy, and you walk up to a girl on the street, and you say, 'Hi, would you like to marry me?' What is she going to say? She's going to think you're nuts, right? You did not follow the appropriate course of action to produce what's called a conversion. There's a process to that. For example, maybe you walk up to her and ask for the time, then ask for her name, then suggest getting coffee, then dinner, and then a movie. Eventually, you're dating, then maybe moving in together, and finally, you can ask, 'Will you marry me?' The same type of conversion system works for sales, and a webinar is essentially a fast track to that conversion."

I told him he needed to change his approach. Instead of asking, "Hey, do you want to pay me $5,000 for a matchmaking service?" he should say, "Hey, I have this free presentation where I'm going to tell you about what's working now in modern dating." Then, during the call, he would lead people on a journey where the only logical conclusion is to join his product or service. By doing so, all those people who initially said, "Why would I ever pay this much money for this?" are what we call "converted." They are now ready to pay for that product or service. So, you went from having a bunch of people saying, "Why the heck would I ever pay this amount of money for this?" to people saying, "Oh my God, there is no other logical explanation than for me to pay this much money for this." And that is the power of having a webinar.

How Webinars Can Transform Businesses

Since 2014, webinars at Marketplace Superheroes have been our number one acquisition channel. We've also used them as our number one upsell channel to upgrade existing clients in our mid-ticket programs (charged anywhere from $500 to $2,000) to offers of $7,000 to $12,000.

We've used webinars to do that.

From a transformation perspective, that's been huge. Another big impact of webinars for us has been the ability to communicate these messages simultaneously in a group setting. For example, when acquiring new clients, it's much easier and better to do so at the $2,000 level on a one-to-many basis instead of having to speak to each customer individually and pay sales commissions to an enrollment person on every sale. In terms of scaling the business faster, webinars have been responsible for some really big, fast-scale moments.

The biggest moment, and what I think was a huge breakthrough, was back in 2015 when we did a webinar with a partner called Jay Boyer. We had our own offer, and in that one webinar campaign, we grossed over $300,000 in sales. This was a huge breakthrough for us because we'd launched the company only the previous year. It was a massive deal: We were able to bring in 300 customers within the space of two weeks, and many of those customers are still with us to this day, ten years later. We've also had backend coaching campaigns where webinars brought in hundreds of thousands of dollars.

One example is a campaign where 43 people took a $12,000 offer from us off the back of a webinar to our audience of buyers once a week.

One of our most emphatic pieces of advice is that you must use scarcity and urgency. And actually, just to back up a bit, not only do you need a great webinar, but you also need a great sequence of emails, text messages, etc. The big lesson here is that most sales are made when you have a sequence. If you only do a live webinar, you're only going to make sales to the people who actually attend the webinar. Let's face it: Nowadays, live webinar attendance rates are anywhere from 10% to 30% on the high side. Evergreen webinars have attendance rates of 30% to 60%.

A mistake I see people make is repeating the same webinar again and again to the same audience without adding new people. This approach is going to burn out relatively quickly. When you have a webinar, you have an asset. You can turn that webinar into a variety of different things. And that's something else to understand—it's not just a webinar.

You can turn it into an ebook, a booking funnel, a Video Sales Letter (VSL), a multi-day challenge, or a product launch. Webinars are a great asset because of their versatility.

A Memorable Webinar With an Unexpected Outcome

Recently, we did a lead magnet swap, where we shared our webinar with a personal finance company. I actually kind of forgot about it. We sent people to an evergreen webinar we created, and we had 326 leads come in, which usually isn't that much for us.

We had 13 sales from that at an average of nearly $2,000 each. So, literally, with nothing to do other than getting a company to send a few emails, we generated around $26,000 within less than 72 hours with no work required. That outcome was really unexpected.

I hope people take away that the offer is critically important. If you can create a great offer and a great webinar, you're going to have outstanding results. If you have a great offer and a not-so-good webinar, you'll still have good results. If you have a not-so-good offer but a great webinar, you're not going to have great results. And if you have a poor offer and a poor webinar, you can forget about it.

Benefits of Running Imperfect Webinars

Not every webinar is going to be perfect. Technology can cause issues, but at the end of the day, people want to connect with people. They don't want to connect with robots or something that seems too polished. I have another colleague in sales who followed all these scripts to a T when selling windows (for buildings, not the operating system). They weren't being themselves and weren't making sales. As soon as they started speaking those scripts in their own authentic tone, they started making a lot of sales. The same idea applies here. We have frameworks, but at the end of the day, you need to inject your own personality into those frameworks.

When you combine that, you get the best of both worlds: Following a proven framework while applying and injecting your personality into it to deliver something where people say, "Wow, this person is being authentic."

That's the power of even an imperfect webinar. This idea speaks to the notion that you don't need to be perfect or perfectly rehearsed. Just have your general framework in mind; the more webinars you do, the better you'll get. If you're not doing a live webinar and are just automating them (more on that later), you don't even have to worry about this as much. The moral of the story is that you don't need to be perfectly scripted on a webinar to get results.

Even just getting on a webinar, connecting with people, and then offering something at the end is going to produce some level of sales. You could probably run a six-figure-a-year business on that alone. But when you put the right things in the right order, it unlocks an even higher tier where you can maximize the number of people buying now and later.

Common Myths About Webinars

As mentioned previously, we want to drive home the point that you can do this. There are a lot of myths associated with webinars, mostly relating to how difficult they are to get up and running. We want to spend some time addressing each of these myths one by one and dispelling them so that you can walk away truly feeling like you're up to the task.

Myth Number One: *Webinars are too time-consuming to create.*
As we outlined earlier, with the right platform and especially the latest advances in AI, getting your webinar up and running from start to finish is easier and faster than ever before.

Myth Number Two: *Webinars require me to be an amazing public speaker.*
Nope. As we touched on earlier, one of the amazing things about webinars is that a little imperfection—a brief pause here, an "um" there—actually comes across as authentic because you're not delivering a super-polished, robotic presentation. You're able to connect with your audience in a way that you could never achieve with just an ad or a regular sales page.

Myth Number Three: *Webinars require me to go live again and again.*
Thanks to technology, this is no longer true. You can automate almost the entire process of getting attendees for your webinar and have them view your pre-recorded webinar presentation. We'll touch on this more fully later on.

Myth Number Four: *I need to be some sort of tech guru or coding expert to set up all the various pieces of my webinar and webinar funnel.*

That's just not true at all. Pick the right platform (we'll discuss this later in this book), and you'll have a tool that is super user-friendly and requires zero technical know-how or coding ability.

Myth Number Five: *This is going to be super expensive.*

Not at all. In fact, it's cheaper than ever to build and run your webinars, and you can even make money from reselling your webinar software if you pick the right platform. But we'll also talk about that later.

Myth Number Six: *Only a small percentage of people can get results with webinars.*

The truth is that most people are using the wrong formula when it comes to webinars. They don't follow the proven order of content we discuss in this book, so they get really poor results. Luckily, you're not in that boat. You have access to this book and our resources, which we give you for free, including our proven webinar script.

Check them out here:

or go to https://getwebinarkit.com/book-resources

Myth Number Seven: *It's too confusing to get started.*

That is simply not true. You will have all you need to create and manage webinars that let you increase sales for your company by the time you finish this book and look through the free resources included in it.

A Webinar With Over-the-Top Benefits

Another quick story about how webinars can easily supercharge your business: I created my first software-as-a-service business, a software with a monthly or yearly subscription. If you've ever tried to sell anything with a recurring price structure, you know it's generally not easy. As a tech guy, I spent months coding and developing my software tool, building a great-looking, slick sales page, preparing for launch, and getting everything put together. I dotted my I's and crossed my T's. But when the day came to launch, reality quickly set in. While I got a few sales from organic traffic and had some success with my affiliate program, sign-ups were pretty slow. I needed a solution fast, as my runway was starting to dry up.

Other people, including Stefan, saw major success with their webinars and businesses. With nothing to lose and limited other prospects for driving immediate growth, I figured, *Why not give webinars a shot?* My affiliate traffic was drying up, paid ads were floundering, and organic traffic was slow. So, I thought to myself, *I can do what they're doing*, and immediately set out to create my first-ever webinar!

I had no clue what I was doing at the time. I simply set out to make a presentation similar to what I saw other people doing. This was back in the day before AI tools were readily available, so it took me a little time to get my webinar up and running. But it really didn't take that long, and it was still pretty easy.

Being the tech guy I am, I'm not much of a public speaker, so I was a little embarrassed to go live in front of an audience with my presentation. I opted to do an automated webinar instead. (Again, we'll touch on the difference between live and automated webinars later in the book.) The day finally came when I was set to start driving traffic and attendees to my first webinar session, and I waited with apprehension to see the results. Thankfully, I was rewarded with success for my hard work, and I almost immediately saw a doubling of my subscription sign-ups and revenue thanks to just the first few webinar sessions I ran. The beauty of it is that those subscribers continued to pay me for years, all from just that one webinar I had developed. It was truly an eye-opening experience for me in many ways. It wasn't just a showcase that anyone can build, run, and succeed with webinars—it also showed that success with my business was actually attainable, even for someone with relatively little marketing experience and who was new to that type of business.

Hopefully, you walk away from this story seeing just how easy it is to get started running webinars that can help you succeed and just how powerful they can be, even for someone who is a complete novice starting out.

CHAPTER 2

The Four-Step Webinar Framework That Turns Cold Leads Into Hungry Buyers

Once you understand this, you have a powerful asset in your business and your industry. What's really cool is that once you memorize this—and it's super easy to understand—your life will change.

You will have the ability to sell anything. With that, we're going to reveal the step-by-step process to show you just how easy it is to do this. So, what are the four actual steps to increase sales in your webinar?

Well, we touched on some of these before, but essentially, the first is your story. Your story is incredibly important because this is how people will relate to you. As much as we all don't like salespeople, we generally do better when we have a relationship with them.

Salespeople know that it's all about building relationships, and the same concept applies to your webinar. You need to build a relationship. If you don't show people who you are, they are not going to trust you as much because you'll come across as just another nameless, faceless person or product trying to sell to them. And that simply doesn't work.

It's why, during sales presentations, simply knowing to call people by their name, asking, "What's your name?" and then using their name over and over again is the first step to getting them to immediately feel more connected to you. So, we're taking that first step and many more steps on this journey.

But in a nutshell, if people don't know who you are, how the heck do you expect them to buy from you? So, on that note, how do we actually tell people the story that optimizes them to buy from us? Well, everyone has a story within them that can be used for whatever it is you're doing. In my webinars, I've had various stories. One of the businesses I had was a Pinterest marketing business. In that business, I sold a course on how other businesses could grow using Pinterest. For that, I had a webinar in which I sold the product. The story for that focused on how I was looking for a way to get more traffic. I talked about how, when I started out with my online businesses, I tried a bunch of different traffic strategies that didn't do well.

For example, I tried search engine optimization, paid ads, etc., and none of those actually worked. Then, I stumbled upon a new traffic method that did incredibly well: Pinterest. I related how this was the thing that helped me overcome all the obstacles that were stopping me from succeeding. The thing I wanted to ultimately achieve, which I talk about in my story, is exactly what the people watching the webinar want to do. So, in a way, the people watching the webinar become you. You become the person in the story. They see a little bit—or a lot—of themselves in you as you're telling the story. You talk about the pain points and issues they're currently facing, and you show them how you found the solution. In the case of Pinterest, these were people who came on a webinar because they saw that their problem was not getting enough traffic, and they needed to find a new solution. They likely tried many of the other traffic strategies I was doing or had heard about them and were afraid to try. By showing them that these other traffic strategies didn't work for me, they could relate.

When I showed them what *did* work, there was more trust immediately because they related to me on what didn't work, so they trusted what did.

That's a huge part of the story. In addition to relating to them on their pain points and goals, you also want to relate to them on a personal level. Show them a bit about who you are. You don't want to come across as some unattainable, hugely famous person because that might turn people off. You're better off showing them that you are a regular person. Share the things you like to do. In my webinars, I like to talk about my *why*. Why do I do the things I do in business? For example, why do I want to run a location-independent business? Well, for me, it's because I want to be able to travel, have location freedom, and do what I want instead of sitting in a cubicle all day. A lot of people can relate to that. Now, I become someone who relates to them not only on their pain points about getting traffic but also on a deeper level about why they need more traffic. When you relate to people on deeper things, you build much more trust.

These are all elements you want to include in your story. When you can successfully do this, at the very least, they're entering the next phase of the webinar framework feeling like you're someone they know, or at minimum, someone with a cool story they can relate to, either partially or fully. You'll have people on the webinar thinking, *Oh my God, this guy is me*, while others might think, *Okay, this guy's kind of cool. I like a lot of what he's saying, I can relate to it.* In either case, you've already built a lot of trust with some people and some trust with a lot of people at this point in the presentation. These are all really powerful pieces, and we dive much deeper into your story in our resources, which you can find at various links throughout this book.

In a nutshell, to summarize the story, start thinking about your journey. Relating to what I said before, your journey or your story can change based on what you're doing. For example, when I'm telling you the story about how I succeeded with webinars, I'm not telling you about Pinterest traffic. I'm telling you about where I struggled in my business to get sales from a different perspective—not getting traffic but improving my sales conversions. That's where webinars came in. So, find the story—the hero's journey, like we were talking about earlier—that relates to what your audience is trying to achieve. Relate to them on that, relate to them on your why, and you'll be well on your way to building a simple story that people can relate to. Again, anyone can do this. I just gave you some great examples of how I've done it in different webinars.

Once you've completed your story, the next thing you want to do is explain what's called the vehicle. So, what do I mean by "the vehicle"? I touched on this a little bit in the story, but essentially, what is the magical thing that solves the problem the person is trying to solve? In the case of my Pinterest webinar, the vehicle was Pinterest traffic. In the case of needing more sales and the sales page not cutting it, the vehicle is a webinar. In each case, what's your vehicle? If you're in the health niche, maybe your vehicle is teaching people how to lose 20 pounds without cutting out certain types of foods. Maybe it's a specific diet where you tell them they don't have to restrict any particular food. That's your vehicle. If you're teaching people how to cure migraines without medication, maybe the vehicle is a particular massage technique. Whatever it is, it's important to think about what solved your problem and the big idea of what you're trying to help someone solve. What is that in your business? What is the vehicle?

Another example: One of my clients had a business where people were looking for something unique that could be run from anywhere in the country with very little competition. The vehicle was an elopement business—helping people plan destination elopements. It was super unique, and it did incredibly well. Your vehicle could be a variety of different things.

Once you introduce that big vehicle, what's going to happen? People are going to have objections to that vehicle. For example, in the case of webinars, what are the things that stop people from taking action on webinars? We talked about this a little bit in the previous chapter: We covered the myths and things that stop people from taking action with webinars that are simply untrue. You want to show people they can actually do this, regardless of what *this* is. Identify the main objections that stop people from taking action on the vehicle you're teaching. For example, with a diet, they might believe, *Oh, I've tried other diets before, and none of them worked.*

Get in front of that objection and learn how to handle it. It's not hard to do. You could sit down right now and come up with ten objections. You could use yourself as an example. Maybe you were your ideal customer at one point. What were the things that stopped you from taking action on something? Write those down and get a list.

It won't take long. You can probably get five to ten objections right now. Then, all you have to do is talk about how those objections are simply untrue. When you handle these objections, you are learning how to stop anyone from deciding not to buy from you. Now, don't get me wrong—there will be people who are so skeptical they'll never buy anything from anyone. But you can get the majority of people to see the value in what you're selling by simply handling five to ten main objections. If you can understand what objections are stopping people and how to get in front of them, you'll be well on your way.

The next part of the framework is called the irresistible offer. So, what exactly is the irresistible offer? When you see something—whether it's a digital or physical product—and the deal is so good that you can't pass it up, you just have to grab it, right? You just have to absolutely grab it. So, how can you make something irresistible?

We just talked about objections. What I like to do in my offers is add everything possible that was an objection as part of the offer. To give you an example, when I was selling my Pinterest traffic product, the main product was a course. It was something you had to go through in video format. The first objection I could think of was that some people wouldn't want to watch videos. So, I created a handy quick-reference PDF for each chapter. You could follow through with the PDF or the videos. By doing this, I handled the objection regarding how people want to consume information.

I anticipated another objection: "Do I have to do this myself?" So, I created what's called the Outsourcing Guide. I taught people how to outsource this for a few dollars an hour to someone, and I even provided them with the Standard Operating Procedures (SOPs) to give to that person so they could do what I was teaching in the course. Now, if someone thought, *This is cool, but I don't want to do it myself*, there was no reason for them not to grab it because they didn't have to do it themselves and didn't have to work hard to train someone else to do it either. Right there, you solve another issue.

Another thing I offered was a "done-for-you" Pinterest profile setup. What does this mean? I told them, "We're going to build your Pinterest profile for you." We would get in there and set it up the right way because some people have another objection: "What if I'm doing this wrong?" So, if you were worried about doing it wrong, we would do it for you. That was another powerful objection taken care of. What's really cool is this webinar ended up converting between 15% and 20% of attendees right on the call to a $1,000 program. That's the power of handling objections.

I want to show you that this is not rocket science. You can absolutely do this. It doesn't take a lot of work. This ties into building your irresistible offer and offering bonuses. I'll give you one more powerful bonus that works extremely well: Always offer a community. People don't want to feel like they need to go at something alone. The majority of people feel, *Oh my God, I'm going to get lost.* They feel like they're alone in a dark room. When you tell them they won't be alone, they'll be in a room filled with others in their shoes, people who might be a little ahead of them or a little behind them, they'll want to be in that room. That's another powerful bonus.

In a nutshell, those are the really big pieces of your webinar. What's really cool is that when you have this format, you can apply it alongside what we like to call "closer techniques." Closer techniques refer to how well you actually sell at the end of the webinar. If you've done your job correctly and followed these four simple steps, you will build your story to get them to know, like, and trust you as a person. You'll explain the vehicle and address every objection you can think of, showing them that this is the solution they've been looking for and that their limiting beliefs around it are simply untrue. You'll present them with an offer that is absolutely irresistible because it includes everything they could possibly need to take action now.

You include every little thing you can think of that might stop them from taking action on that offer. By the end, they'll think, *Oh my God, I can't even think of anything at this point that would stop me from getting this.* What do you do at this point?

We have some powerful techniques that can help you convert at even higher rates. We call these closer techniques, too. One of the closer techniques we really like and have used on our webinars is called the "20-minute timer." This is really powerful because when you do a live webinar, you can go in and offer what's called a "fast-action bonus," limit the quantity of something, double the amount of something you're offering, or lower the price of something. You can experiment and see what works best, but you essentially say, "For the next 20 minutes, we're going to give you this if you get in now. If you're going to be an action taker, you're going to get this bonus by doing so." You start the timer, and lo and behold, watch as people scramble to get in line to buy because they see that timer ticking while you're answering questions, and they want to get in. The 20-minute timer is incredibly effective.

The timer creates urgency, but you can also use scarcity. For example, "For the next five people, we're going to give you this epic bonus," or "For the next seven people, we're going to give you this epic bonus." When you do this, people jump at the opportunity. They're going to think, *Oh my God, I need to get this before someone else does.* It creates major FOMO (Fear of Missing Out) because you created scarcity. Scarcity has been ingrained in human DNA since the dawn of time. People want something more when there is a limited amount. You can leverage that to sell much more on your webinars. These are two extremely powerful closer techniques that will really help you boost your sales.

In a nutshell, if you can understand these four things we just talked about—and we have a lot of resources to make this incredibly easy for you, even leveraging the power of AI to do so in our resources—you'll be set.

Product Launch Before and After the Framework

Now, time for a quick case study example. We're actually going to talk about our experience in a situation where we launched a new product via a webinar *before* we used this framework and *after* we used this framework.

Stefan and I were launching a brand-new product years ago, and of course, we launched it via a webinar. We were super excited to launch this new product, as we had worked extremely hard on it and were proud of what we had created. We thought it was going to be a big success at first, but upon launching it, it was actually a massive flop. We were dismayed and confused. The product was great. What the heck happened?

We realized we weren't following a proper framework in so many different ways. We weren't telling a story that allowed our audience to relate to us and that also showcased or clarified how our irresistible offer would be helpful to them.

We were sort of showing the vehicle to their success, but it was overly confusing and complicated. Our offer, which we thought was irresistible, was just downright confusing—people didn't even know what they were buying.

We weren't utilizing proper webinar closing techniques, which are almost guaranteed to boost your webinar sales and conversions. So, we took some time to figure out what happened and went back to the drawing board. Literally, just a day or two later, we simplified our story. We made it more concise, clear, and to the point for our audience. We clarified the vehicle to the attendee's success so that they understood what we were actually talking about.

As a result, our irresistible offer made more sense, and people knew what we were selling. Lastly, we started to sprinkle in some high-converting webinar closing techniques that massively boosted our sales and conversions.

What happened? We immediately saw a massive difference in sales. We went from literally zero sales to one of our best-converting, highest-performing products ever. This is just a simple case study of how applying this powerful framework can turn cold, skeptical leads into hungry buyers begging to pay you.

CHAPTER 3

How to Get Content for Your Webinar in Minutes Even if You Don't Know Where to Start

You're in for a real treat with this chapter. Some people are absolutely terrified of building a webinar. They think it takes a long time to find the content, or that they need to do a ton of pre-work, and that it might take them as long as a year to get it done. I'm here to tell you, for a period of time in my career, this was true.

It often took me six months or more to complete a webinar. The little things always took forever. You follow the slide framework, get through about five to ten slides, and think, *Okay, things are going pretty well.* Then you get to slide 15 and realize *This is taking longer than expected.* By the time you reach slide 25, you're exhausted and see that you're only 25% of the way done. And when you finally finish 100 or so slides, you're thinking to yourself, *I can't believe I have to go through and edit this again and find the errors.* You end up continuing to polish something that could take six months to finish.

What's really cool is that I'm a little jealous of you because, at this point, you don't need to do any of that. Nope, you don't need to do a single thing I just described. You don't need to suffer for six months or more to complete a webinar.

Now, you can actually create a webinar in as little as a few minutes—or, at the very least, the content for it—thanks to the power of AI. You've probably heard of this by now, but you may not have seen the full extent of its power when it comes to growing your business in record time. So, how does AI help you grow your business so quickly?

It all starts with something called a "customer avatar." The first thing you need to do is identify your customer avatar. What's really cool is that you can use AI to get everything you need to define your customer avatar. The first step is to use our customer avatar sheet, which is available as a resource in this book, to determine who your customer avatar is. All you have to do is fill out our form—it takes about 5 minutes—and you'll have a very good idea about who you're selling to. One thing I've learned in my marketing career, even as a very advanced marketer, is that success often comes back to having a deep understanding of your customer avatar. We sometimes think the solution is complex, but it often boils down to refining our understanding of our target audience. If you're reading this, you're on the right track by starting with your customer avatar.

Once you have your customer avatar, you can use AI tools to get all the information you need about them. By information, I mean who they are as a person and everything I discussed related to the hero's journey in the previous section. For example, what are their reasons? What are their pain points unrelated to business, or what specific problem are they trying to solve? What are their goals? What are their big-picture reasons and pain points?

For instance, if you're a chiropractor, your customer avatar might be a guy named John who is dealing with lower back pain. His big-picture goal is to get out of pain so he can play catch with his kids or travel the world. The specific action he needs to take might be an exercise to relieve his back pain. He doesn't really want to do the exercise, but he does it because it will help him achieve his bigger goal.

This is the framework for understanding a customer avatar. When you grasp this, you have everything you need to create a really effective webinar using the power of AI. By using the resources we provide, you can generate a detailed analysis of your customer avatar, identifying their exact pain points. Trust me, this can get extremely deep. You're not just going for surface-level pain points. You want people on your webinar to think, *How did they know? How did they know I'm dealing with [XYZ]?* When you can reach that level of depth, people will really relate to and trust you because you've articulated their struggles exactly.

Once you have this deep understanding of your customer avatar, you can use AI to create an amazing starting point. We explain how to do this in minutes with AI in our resources. From there, you can use certain AI tools, such as Claude.AI, to upload items and train the AI on them.

For example, you can upload a PDF version of a book. You can also upload a webinar template. One of the amazing gifts we provide in this book is our proven webinar template, which uses the formula we discussed in the previous chapter. This template has been optimized over years of running effective sales webinars to grow various businesses.

You can take that webinar template, upload it into Claude.AI, and train the AI to create your webinar slide by slide. The AI will understand the framework and know what to do. You've now done two things with AI that we show you in our resources: You've identified your customer avatar, so the AI knows who you're targeting, and you've uploaded your webinar template. Then you can tell the AI, "You now understand who my customer avatar is, you understand what we're selling to them, and you understand how to create a conversion-optimized webinar based on this slide template. Now, go ahead and write my webinar slide by slide for me." You will be amazed at how far AI has come in writing a conversion-optimized webinar.

I've tried this for a few of our more recent projects, and I was absolutely blown away by what the AI came up with. The sales angles it generated—even with my 10-plus years of copywriting experience—were things I couldn't have thought of in a million years. I was able to combine my current knowledge with what the AI provided to create an even more powerful sales presentation in record time. That's why I'm jealous of you—because you're starting here. You get to use AI to build extremely effective sales presentations in record time and understand your customer avatar better than ever before.

From there, you get the content, and what's really cool is that you can tell the AI to give you the content slide by slide, formatted for a designer. You can either design the slides yourself or hand them off to a freelancer to have an amazing webinar presentation ready faster than ever.

If you're really focused, this process dramatically reduces the time compared to sitting there and pulling your hair out to gather all this information manually. Now, if you don't want to use AI and prefer to do this manually, we've still made it ridiculously easy for you—as easy as it could be without using AI—because we provide all the resources you need. All you have to do is plug in the information. Either way, the amount of time it will take you to do this the right way and achieve high conversions will be dramatically reduced.

Once you've done this, you'll have all the content you need. At this point, it couldn't get any easier to have a conversion-optimized webinar ready to go. In addition to that, what's really cool is that you don't have to use this process just for your webinar. Obviously, when you run a webinar, you'll need emails around that webinar: emails that invite people to the webinar, emails that remind them to show up, and emails after the webinar letting people know about the replay and the products or services you're selling.

We'll be talking more about those pieces later on. They're pretty straightforward. But what's really cool is that we also provide some email resources. For example, you can upload email templates—ours or anyone else's—into Claude.AI and say, "Okay, great, now write the emails that go along with this webinar." Now you've got your marketing materials—not just the webinar, but also the other marketing materials. Just like that, you've used the power of AI to build an incredibly detailed customer avatar, a high-converting webinar presentation, and the supporting marketing materials you need to get this webinar out there.

At this point, I'm more excited than ever for you to get your first webinar going and start generating more sales than you ever thought possible.

CHAPTER 4

How to Launch Your Webinar in Record Time Without Technical Skills

In this chapter, we'll cover how to launch your webinar as fast as humanly possible without the frustration of spending hours trying and failing to get the various pieces of your webinar working together exactly the way you want. So far in the book, we've covered the power of webinars. You understand the concept behind why they work, the essential elements you need, and how to gather all the content for your actual presentation. Now, the next step is to actually build your webinar funnel. Luckily for you, we've made it easy.

Sometimes, the terms "webinar" and "webinar funnel" are used interchangeably, but typically, the webinar funnel refers to the complete package of everything related to your webinar. This includes the registration/landing page, the thank you page, the watch room where people actually view your presentation, and what's often referred to as the replay page. On the other hand, "webinar" often refers just to the presentation and its content. In this chapter, we'll focus more on how to launch your webinar funnel in record time and all the various components that go into it.

You're probably familiar with the term funnel in the context of marketing, but just as a super quick recap. It's similar to an actual funnel, where at the top of the funnel, you have a wider opening, and at the bottom, stuff exits from a narrower spout. Applying that cooking analogy to your webinar funnel, at the top, you have your registration page to which people can be directed from various traffic sources like paid ads, organic social media posts, affiliate traffic, and more. As people register for your webinar and watch your presentation, they're moving through your webinar funnel. Generally, for most people who run webinars, the end goal is that these registrants become customers and buy your products or services as they reach the bottom of your funnel. So, when we say "webinar funnel," we're generally referring to the combination of elements like your registration page, where people can register for a webinar session from a list of times; a thank you page after they register for your event, with simple instructions and perhaps a call to action; the actual watch room page, where people watch your webinar presentation itself; and optionally, a replay page, where people who missed the scheduled session can view the presentation on-demand for a specified period of time.

Now, you might think, *This is a lot of stuff going on. I'm going to need some tech skills here. I'm going to need to code some of this stuff to link everything together,* but we're here to tell you that nothing could be further from the truth!

In fact, it's faster than ever to get set up thanks to the latest advances in technology and AI, as we've mentioned throughout this book. With all that said, let's continue.

You're going to need some sort of tool to build your webinar funnel. We, of course, recommend using the one we built ourselves and use in our own business: WebinarKit. We built it to work perfectly with our whole webinar formula, making everything we're discussing here easy to set up and follow. We also added features we couldn't find in other tools at the time, like replay pages and embeddable webinar rooms, so you can paste an entire webinar on your own website. You are, of course, welcome to use any tool you want, but you can check ours out for a $1 trial on our website, getwebinarkit.com.

People like to overcomplicate things. You can spend time optimizing things—and you should in time—but the truth is, you're better off starting simple, getting in your reps, and then improving from there.

To start, all you really need is:

- **Your webinar registration page.** This is where you'll collect prospects' contact info before sending them to the webinar.
- **The thank you page.** The page they land on after registering, confirming their spot, with details on how to watch the webinar.
- **The webinar watch room.** Where they view the webinar presentation, live or automated (more on that later). This is where we build our audience of people who know, like, and trust us, and where we get our first buyers.
- **The replay page.** For people who couldn't attend live. People lead busy lives these days.
- **The follow-ups.** This is where we keep following up with people, staying top of mind, and continuously selling and bringing in sales.

If you can get *this* done, you are there. This is a funnel that produces sales, provided you fill those pieces with the *right* information, which we're going to show you how to do here.

Now, what do we actually put on each of these pages?

Just as you can leverage AI to build out your entire webinar presentation content, you can do the same thing for your registration, thank you, and replay pages, thanks to the latest advances in AI. You can easily leverage tools like ChatGPT or Claude AI.

Some tools even come with powerful AI features built right into the software to generate text that you can seamlessly insert into your pages in literally just seconds.

Now let's quickly talk about the first page we mentioned, the registration page, also known as the landing page, which is essentially what collects webinar registrants' contact info/emails, allowing you to contact them in the future for other webinars or remarketing. The registration page, also commonly known as a landing page for your webinar, is one of the most important components of your webinar funnel.

This can make or break everything because this is where people will typically sign up for your webinar presentations so they can view and hear your content. But it's more than just someone picking a time and date to view your presentation. When they sign up for your webinar, you're getting their contact details, typically a name, an email address, and potentially even a phone number.

If you have any experience with marketing whatsoever, you probably already know how valuable this is. When you have someone's contact details—and, depending on your location or country, their consent to send them marketing messages—you can follow up with them and continue marketing to them long after the webinar presentation they signed up for is over. Even if that person doesn't convert during your webinar presentation, they might convert on the replay of your webinar, the next webinar after that, or somewhere further down the line. That's why this might arguably be considered the most important part of the webinar funnel, believe it or not—even if the person who registers on your landing page doesn't show up to the session they initially registered for.

Registration Page

After learning about the registration page and its significance, let us discuss the essential elements that any successful webinar landing page or registration page should have:

1. **Catchy, compelling headline or sub-headline.** Encourage prospective registrants to register. Why should they be spending their valuable time on your presentation? For instance, "The new strategy supercharging results this year" or "How I did X that massively grew my business in Y time." This headline, which makes it obvious why they should attend, should be the most alluring aspect of your event.

2. **The registration form and call to action are clearly visible.** Add a form for information such as name, email address, and phone number, along with a noticeable "Register Now" button. Make sure it is above the fold and simple to modify so users can see it right away without having to scroll.

3. **Secrets and advantages.** Include bullet points or a brief paragraph outlining additional advantages or secrets they will discover. These ought to support your primary headline or subheadline.

4. **Section for presenters.** Before the event, introduce yourself. Include a picture of the presenter to help registrants get to know you.

5. **Countdown clock.** A countdown timer increases urgency and makes sure registrants know when the next session begins, both of which are critical for sales and conversions.

6. **More Components:**
    - **Video Recordings.** A strong video can build interest and encourage more people to sign up.
    - **Testimonials.** Utilize client and attendee testimonials as social proof.
    - **The Design.** Make sure the page displays well on tablets, smartphones, and desktop computers.
    - **Contact Details.** You can gather email addresses and phone numbers. By focusing on these elements, you can build a registration page that can often convert as much as 50% or more of the visitors into registrants, giving you the opportunity to get their contact information and offer them marketing until they depart!

Thank You Page

Next up, after the registration page, we have the thank you page, including some tricks of the trade we've learned over 7-plus years of webinar marketing to make it work way better. This is where people are directed immediately after registering for your event, another important component of your webinar funnel. Here, you'll give the registrant simple instructions so they know how to watch your presentation, when the presentation is, and how to join the presentation watch room. It can also be a great place to engage a little bit more with your registrants before the main content and presentation. You can offer a little bit more about you or the presenter, what they'll be learning, and reinforce all the benefits of attending.

Additionally, here's something that transformed our webinar funnels by really taking our thank you page power to the next level. In addition to confirming their spot on the webinar, give them an action to take in the meantime. For example, you can ask them to join your community, book a call with you or your team, or even pitch them some sort of low-ticket, tripwire offer that can help potentially recoup things like paid ad spend before they even show up to your main event, where you pitch them your main product or offer. The idea here is that the whole purpose of a webinar is to get them to take action with you toward a purchase. Some percentage of registrants are ready to do that before the webinar, so why deprive them of the option? Whether you book calls from the thank you page, get them into a community, or sell some lower-priced product to recoup ad spend, you can't go wrong. Maximizing the thank you page real estate with this step will show results quickly and change your funnel trajectory forever.

What else ought to be included on a thank you page besides this tip?

1. **Easy directions to your presentation.** Verify that attendees understand how to watch your presentation. In the case of just-in-time webinars or instant watch, inform them that the session will start shortly.
2. **A countdown timer.** Whether in seconds or days, a countdown timer notifies registrants when the session begins.
3. **The unique link for the webinar.** Each registrant is given a unique session link by a good platform. This link ought to take them straight to the thank-you page or the presentation room. For future access, make sure emails include this link.
4. **Calendar and links to social media.** Make it simple for attendees to share the event on social media and add it to their calendar. This is easy with platforms like WebinarKit.
5. **Benefits of the event and more information about you.** Tell them again why they signed up and the advantages of going. As a reminder, this could resemble the information on your registration page.

6. **Make a low-ticket offer an option.** You can offer them a bonus for signing up or invite them to join your social media community. This is a great way to interact with them more.

Enhancements:
- **A video message.** To increase authority and rapport, thank registrants and describe the next steps.
- **Reviews.** Display more testimonies to establish credibility.

Follow our tips, and you'll have a thank you page that does everything it needs to do and then some.

Webinar Watch Room

From there, the next component is where they view the actual webinar presentation: the webinar watch room.

This is where the registrant becomes the attendee. This is where your leads actually watch your presentation, and this is where the magic of webinars really starts to happen. In the webinar watch room, they'll see your curated presentation that will let you speak in a one-to-many fashion, all the while massively building rapport, connecting and engaging with your audience, establishing authority, holding your audience's attention for potentially hours, and allowing you to deliver your pitch in the exact way you want.

Although the watch room is not as complicated as many other pages, you should optimize a few things to get the best results:

1. **Video of exceptional quality.** Make sure your video is clear, high-quality, and front and center. Steer clear of sending viewers to YouTube, where you are vying for their attention. You can upload and have your video play automatically on platforms like

WebinarKit, which preserves the feel of a live event. Make sure your platform can pick up where the user left off in case they switch devices or refresh.

2. **Chat in real time.** By enabling attendees to communicate with you and one another, a live chat box increases engagement and conversions. You can provide real-time answers to questions even in automated webinars, giving you the "best of both worlds."

3. **Box for questions.** Add a question box via email for webinars that are completely automated. This enables viewers to email questions and get answers in real time.

4. **Features of engagement.** Encourage participation by using surveys and handouts to keep participants' attention on your presentation, which raises conversion rates and revenue.

5. **Visual offerings.** In your pitch, emphasize your product with visual offers. It should be simple for viewers to check out your offer with this section's attention-grabbing text, call to action, and possibly a product image.

6. **Webinar Brand.** To keep brand awareness high, display your colors and logo in the webinar room. Select an application such as WebinarKit that enables you to design the space while concealing its logo.

7. **Simulator for chat.** During automated webinars, the use of simulated chat messages can increase participation. Replay past live chats, welcome guests, and drop offer links with them. It is ethical to point out that it is a replay of an earlier event to increase the perceived level of engagement.

By incorporating these elements, you create a high-quality, engaging webinar experience that keeps viewers focused and boosts conversions. All of these components bundled together can make your webinar watch room a super-focused area where the viewer is locked in on your presentation. They're not getting distracted by clickbait video thumbnails, like on YouTube, for example, or the next post/reel on Instagram and Facebook.

They're dialed into your content, engaging with the live chat or asking questions in the question box. They're answering polls, seeing and clicking on your offers during your product pitches, and seeing exclusively your brand in the watch room, along with messages from you or even simulated chat replies, thanks to the chat simulator.

All of these things come together to create a much greater experience than simply directing people to a YouTube link or a simple video on a webpage. So now you see all the pieces that make a great webinar watch room, and hopefully, you're walking away with a clear idea of what you want in your webinar platform.

Webinar Replay Page

Next, you will want a simple page with a headline, video, and button as the replay page. You will mail this to people who registered but didn't buy.

Follow-up Emails & Text Messages

Follow-up emails, text messages, and event reminders before and during the event are crucial components of your webinar funnel. One way to ensure high attendance rates is with email and text message reminders.

These reminders typically include unique session links so attendees can easily access your presentation. This is good for engagement, keeping attendees involved before, during, and after the webinar with relevant updates and information.

It's beneficial to add personalization to these messages wherever possible to make attendees feel valued and appreciated. Having all this automated and set up so that you're not manually sending out reminders and text messages for an upcoming webinar is crucial. Any good webinar platform, like WebinarKit, will allow you to do this automatically.

In addition to event reminders, follow-up emails and text messages are important because they allow you to send people to a replay page. Anyone who missed your "live" event can be redirected automatically to a replay page where they can view your webinar content on-demand. This can often literally double your conversions and sales.

One last secret is something called the "textinar." These are follow-up reminders during the webinar itself that ensure your audience is showing up and engaging with your webinar. Even though the webinar is starting, they'll get a text message that the event is ongoing, prompting them to join immediately.

Another powerful tool can be a webinar encore. This is something you can insert after your webinar event and before the replay page. If it's a live webinar, you just run it again. If automated, you send them back to the watch room. It can be later the same day or the next day. The messaging can be as simple as "Hey, we're doing an encore presentation on ___ at ___. If you missed the first one or loved it so much that you want to attend again, come join us!"

Remember, you can leverage AI for all of this.

Leveraging AI to build out your various pages' content—either using dedicated services like ChatGPT or Claude AI or with a webinar platform that has these AI features built-in, like WebinarKit—can be extremely helpful. This will allow you to quickly generate content for your various pages without stressing about whether it will be high-converting enough.

These AI tools have advanced greatly and can be super helpful in allowing you to create high-quality copy for your various pages so that you get the maximum number of registrants and attendees—and eventually, buyers—for whatever it is you're selling or offering.

Summary

If you can get these simple pages set up, you're almost there:
- A registration page
- A thank you page
- A watch room page
- A replay page
- Follow-ups

That's enough to convert, provided you fill in the pages with the information we talked about. From here, you've got your presentation and your funnel. Now, how do you actually present your webinar?

CHAPTER 5

How to Present Your Webinar for Maximum Sales Without Stage Fright

Ok, great! You have your first webinar funnel, and your slides are done. What's next?

The good news is that presenting on a webinar is not that hard. And if you never want to go live, you're really going to love what we talk about in the next chapter. For now, though, whether you go live or not, make sure you pay close attention to this chapter. We share powerful tools to maximize your revenue and results from the webinar funnel.

The Mindset to Take When Speaking on Your Webinar

When I first started doing webinars, I wasn't really sure how to promote and speak effectively on them. My first few webinars were super professional, but I was a bit dry—almost like a college professor. I remember thinking to myself, *I hated sitting through lectures when I was in college, so why would anyone want to sit through this type of webinar?* Then, I realized something: I needed to be more engaging and entertaining.

Movies are interactive, and people love watching them because they're entertaining, right? I realized that I needed to bring that same energy to my webinars. Here's the thing: Anyone can be entertaining, and I'm going to give you a simple formula to do it right now. It's as easy as thinking about your closest friends and how you interact with them. When you hang out, talk on the phone, or go on a trip, you're just being yourself—natural, making jokes, and free-flowing. The people closest to you understand your personality, and that's why they enjoy your company.

Now, think about someone you don't have a close relationship with, like a college professor or a boring coworker. You don't have a connection with them, and you find them kind of boring, so you don't really want to speak to that person. I want you to think about how you can speak on a webinar the way you do with your closest friends. Imagine you're on the back porch with a friend, sipping a beer or cocktail, having a conversation. Think about a topic you've discussed in the past—often, the topic of your webinar is something you're passionate about and have talked about with someone before.

I recently had coffee with a friend who's starting a business teaching Brazilian jiu-jitsu online. He was casually talking to me, saying, "You know, it's so crazy. Brazilian jiu-jitsu changed my life. It gave me confidence, helped me meet my wife, and allowed me to do all these amazing things." I looked at him and said, "Do you realize you just gave your webinar presentation to me without even knowing it?" He was stunned. The energy and passion in his casual conversation made me almost want to try Brazilian jiu-jitsu, even though I'm not the target audience.

I've had similar casual conversations with friends about the importance of having a webinar in their business, and I've convinced nearly all of them to implement one, just by being myself and talking about the benefits casually. If you want to know how to present at a webinar, start by thinking about the topic you're discussing. Hopefully, you believe in it enough to be passionate about the benefits, and then think about how you'd explain it to a friend on the back porch while enjoying a drink. You don't have to be a comedian; you just have to be a human with some passion and energy behind what you're talking about. That's all it takes to convince the person on the other end.

Picture yourself on the back porch, talking to a friend, amazed by the topic and its power—just like my friend explaining how Brazilian jiu-jitsu changed his life. If you can do that, you'll be able to present your webinars in the best possible way.

Another thing to consider when presenting your webinar: You don't want it to be a one-sided conversation. Nobody likes a friend who talks for two hours without letting you get a word in, even if they're super entertaining. So, engage your audience the same way you'd engage a friend in a conversation. Polls and handouts are two powerful ways to engage your audience on a webinar.

Polls are fun because they serve two purposes. First, they engage the audience and make sure they're paying attention to your "movie" (your webinar). Second, they give you a pulse on where people are and allow you to gather data. Handouts are another great tool. Throughout the webinar, you can use handouts to incentivize people to stay until the end. For example, offer a special handout that doubles their results if they stay until the end. You can also give out random handouts as gifts during the presentation, like saying, "If you're paying attention, put a 2 in the chat, and I'll send a handout to those who do." This re-engages your audience and makes them feel seen and heard.

These little touches make your webinar feel more like a conversation than a lecture. Think of it like a comedy show where the comedian interacts with the audience and brings people up on stage. The more your audience feels like part of the experience, the more likely they are to buy from you. All of these features are built into WebinarKit, making it super easy for you to maximize your sales with these powerful tools.

If you can apply everything you've learned in this chapter—from building a simple funnel to presenting your webinar—you're well on your way to dramatically growing your business.

The Power of Urgency

As discussed previously, urgency has been incredibly effective in our entrepreneurial careers. The concept is simple: You want to get people to take action now, not later. To do that, you need to create some form of urgency. In webinars, this can take the form of an on-webinar bonus for people who opt into your offer before the webinar ends, a pricing discount, or perhaps either of those before the replay ends. A timer can be used on the webinar itself (it's super easy to embed a timer on a Google Slide presentation), and tools usually have built-in countdown timers you can add in the watch room or on replay pages or offer pages after the webinar presentation.

In general, repeatedly reminding people about urgency will help maximize sales. This can be the difference between a 3% conversion rate and a 30% conversion rate. I highly recommend leveraging it. Additionally, make sure you never use fake urgency.

The Power of Scarcity

Scarcity is like urgency's cousin and is also extremely powerful. The concept is simple: Get people to take action now, not by limiting time, but by limiting the amount. Perhaps you have a special bonus and want to give it to the first ten people only. Or you could tier the pricing: the first five people get one price, and the next five get another. This way, people want to act quickly for fear of missing out on one of the limited items. The same concept applies when presenting: Remind people about this as often as possible during the selling portion of the webinar.

Want More Sales? Stay on the Webinar Longer

As you go through your slide deck template provided in our resources, you'll do your main pitch and then get to the final slide where the offer is, possibly accompanied by a timer. This is where you'll start answering everyone's questions. But what do you do when you've answered most of the questions, or you don't have many left? Simple: Start the pitch again from the top.

People have short attention spans. On webinars, it's very hard to be too redundant. You need to keep reminding people of your offer, how great it is, and any urgency or scarcity. Run through it again, and when you finish the last slide, go back to the questions. Provided there are enough people on the call, you should have new questions coming in. In general, the longer you stay on the webinar, the more sales you'll make. If you have the time, run through it a third time. Talk to people about personal stuff, such as how your day is going, and ask them questions, too.

Call People Out by Name

There's a powerful strategy that works well on webinars: calling people out by name. When you speak to someone directly and use their name, it builds a connection quickly.

At the beginning of the webinar, greet everyone by name and ask where they're from. If they chat, talk to them directly. Address everyone: "Welcome, John, Bobby, Gina, etc." "Oh, you're from Australia? Wow, I went there last year!" Toward the end of the webinar, I'll start calling out attendees by name again: "John, Karla, Bobby… I want to help you! Let me know your questions."

In conclusion, don't overthink the presentation of webinars. Be yourself—that's what people connect with. With some basic practice, you can find the right energy to hold. Follow the steps we laid out here to sell like a champion. From there, either pre-record your webinar video using a screen recording tool or get ready to hold your first live webinar. If you want to automate webinars fully and are nervous about having to give live webinars all the time, you're really going to like the next chapter.

CHAPTER 6

How Your Webinar Can Generate Sales Repeatedly Without Needing to Go On Live

The Power of Automated Webinars

When I first started running webinars in my business, I used to do a bunch of live webinars on the back end of what we would call product launches. These were low-priced information products that we would sell, generating a lot of sales all at once, and then we'd funnel those buyers into a live webinar. I was always so nervous about those live webinars, and one of the things we dealt with regularly during them was technical issues. Often, things would go wrong—like the internet connection dropping, forgetting certain things I needed to say at specific times, and even an instance where we had hundreds of people on a webinar, and one of the presenters accidentally closed the entire session. This meant that hundreds of potential customers, ready to purchase something worth thousands of dollars, were lost. This is the downside of live webinars—not only can they be extremely tiring and difficult to run from a technological perspective, but they also introduce potential problems that could cause you to lose a lot of money.

That's when I eventually discovered automated webinars. What I loved about automated webinars was that I could pre-record a presentation, upload it to run at a specific time, and have the presentation run flawlessly while still maintaining a live feel by engaging with people in the chat. With automated webinars, the risk of technical issues, blunders, or someone accidentally ending the session is drastically reduced. You have a nearly perfect presentation every time, and all you need to do is engage with people in the chat, which gives them the feeling of being seen and heard, maintaining the live atmosphere.

Another great aspect of automated webinars is that you can still create a recording that feels very live and human. As we've discussed in previous chapters, it's crucial to come across as a human being, not a robot or a boring college professor. With a recording, you can achieve this while enjoying the flexibility that automated webinars offer.

If you're scared of going live and terrified of running live webinars, I want to reassure you that live webinars still have their place and are great for various purposes. We use a lot of hybrid webinars in our business now, and we'll share more about those later. But the beauty is that if you really don't want to do live webinars, you don't have to. You can automate everything by simply recording your webinar.

What's even cooler is that if you don't want to record the webinar yourself, you can hire someone else to do it for you. I have many colleagues who use webinars in their businesses, and some of them, particularly those from other countries selling primarily to the American market, hire presenters with American accents to record the webinar. They worry that their own accents might negatively affect conversions, so they find a way to overcome that hurdle. I'm not saying that this is something that you have to go out and do. I'm simply illustrating that there are people who are dealing against the odds and are still going out there and running automated webinars by finding all the ways to do it.

Another really powerful thing about automated webinars is that you don't have to rely on having a big launch or a large amount of traffic for a launch. One thing with live webinars is that they always start at a specific date or time, which means that if you can't get a lot of traffic in a certain amount of time, you might be worried that you're going to go live for two hours and then no one's going to buy anything. What's really cool is that you can use automated webinars to dip your toe into testing a product or service and how it's converting.

Maybe you only get 50 people to RSVP for a webinar over the course of a week. But if just one of those 50 people buys something worth $3,000, you have a pretty good conversion rate and know that your webinar converts. You can then take that webinar, run it live the following week with the same or more traffic, and potentially see even more sales. Automated webinars are a great way to start small, get something out there, and build up to big profits without the stress of going live or dealing with the challenges that come with it.

As I mentioned earlier in the book, when I (Phil) was just getting started with a new business, I turned to webinars as the solution. It ultimately ended up being a great success for me, but I did have some reservations at the time.

Hopefully, by sharing my prior hesitations with you and showing you that there was nothing to be worried about, you'll feel more confident if you're having any doubts or reservations about webinars or presenting webinar content.

Public speaking has never been one of my strong suits. I'm more of the tech guy when it comes to business, so speaking in front of a group and presenting webinar content wasn't something I looked forward to. As I was creating my first webinar, I worried about messing up during the presentation, blathering like an idiot, or freezing up. But thankfully, as we're showing you in this chapter, presenting webinars in a completely automated manner is 100% doable. Alternatively, as mentioned before, you can get the best of both worlds by presenting a pre-recorded video during your automated webinar while responding and interacting with attendees live in the chat—commonly known as a hybrid webinar.

For someone who isn't particularly fond of speaking in front of large audiences, this was perfect when I started out with webinars. I could focus on making a solid pre-recorded presentation without worrying about delivering it live in front of a large virtual audience. Once I had my automated webinar set up and had performed a few live webinars, I gained the confidence to start running live webinars later on. But the beauty is that the choice is fully yours when it comes to how you want to deliver your presentation.

In addition to calming my fears of making a fool of myself in front of a large audience, automated webinars are just way more convenient compared to live webinars. That was certainly the case with my first webinar for my business. When I found out that not only did automated webinars allow me to skip the public speaking part entirely but also deliver my presentation without me doing any live work and being able to sell around the clock on autopilot, it was like an answer delivered to me on a silver platter. That's why I personally love automated webinars.

A reservation that some people might have with automated webinars is being worried about the automated nature of it all. They think, *Is this dishonest? Don't people know it's not live?* And really, it all comes down to how you present your content during the webinar. In general, when it comes to automated webinars, there are definitely ethical ways to present pre-recorded content. For example, if you're running a webinar, we generally don't recommend trying to fake things and make it seem like it's a live event. For example, don't welcome completely fake or made-up participants during your intro, or use tools like the chat simulator to drop in fake attendee chat messages to show fake engagement from your audience. Generally, with automated webinars, a better way to handle things is by making it clear that you're the admin, saying something like, "Hey, we're live here in the chat to answer your questions," or "You can send us questions via the questions box or questions form, and we'll respond to you ASAP." You can have the chat simulator drop those messages from you or the moderator in an automated manner so that you don't have to do that work. But on top of that, in general, if you don't make a big fuss over the event being live when it's not or try to fake engagement, most people aren't going to even care in the first place.

It's when people think they're being blatantly lied to that things can get problematic, and people can get upset, which is why we don't recommend trying to make your automated pre-recorded video seem like a fully live event. If you want, you can even take things a step further and disclose upfront to the attendees that they're watching pre-recorded content, but an actual human being is manning the live chat or questions box. That choice is up to you. Another method you can use is saying upfront that they're watching a replay of a prior live event. This ties together nicely when you're using simulated chat messages to display chat messages from a previous real webinar with real attendee messages.

That leads us to ethical chat simulation. Now, you might be thinking, with regards to simulated chat messages, *What is the point of this feature if I can't use it to "fake" attendee chat messages?* Well, there are actually plenty of valid uses for the chat simulator. For example, one great use can be automating live chat messages that you or your live chat moderators would manually send in the first place. For example, you could welcome people to the webinar in the live chat and let them know that you or your team will see their questions. Depending on the type of automated event you're running, you can either respond immediately or after a short delay. Whether you have someone available to manage the live chat in real time or you're using automated messages through a chat simulator, you can prompt users to answer a poll or download the handout you've just shared in the webinar watch room. And, of course, one of the best use cases is for automatically dropping your offer links in the live chat while you're pitching your product during the presentation.

That can be really powerful because, again, your attendees don't have to manually type in your link in the browser—people are lazy. They can just click the link that pops up for them in the chat. So that's definitely a totally valid use case of chat simulation and definitely an ethical way to do it. But another totally ethical and super effective use case for chat simulation is for a webinar replay. So essentially, again, you can disclose upfront in your presentation or registration page that the attendee is viewing a replay of a live event.

From there, you can use an existing list of real chat messages from a previous live event and load them into your webinar watch room, depending on the tool you're using, such as WebinarKit. This allows the attendees to experience the real engagement that occurred during the original live event, effectively transferring some of that live energy to the automated webinar. This approach can be both highly effective and ethical for your automated webinars. So, as long as you take the right approach in presenting yourself during these webinars, you don't need to worry about them being unethical or dishonest at all.

Moving on to some interesting data regarding live versus automated webinars, which you're likely to find insightful. As the founders of WebinarKit, Stefan and I have access to real-world data on this topic, and the results may encourage you to explore automated webinars further. According to our usage data from WebinarKit, 50% of registrants actually attend the automated webinars they sign up for. In contrast, only about 30% of registrants attend live webinars. That's a significant difference. So, why is there such a disparity? While this involves a bit of theorizing, a major factor is likely the immediate or 'just in time' availability of automated webinars—meaning they can be watched within a few minutes or even instantly after registering. It makes intuitive sense: If someone registers and can watch right away, they're more likely to do so. On the other hand, while offering benefits like potentially better audience engagement, live events often suffer from busy registrants forgetting about the event or simply losing interest by the time it starts. Automated webinars capitalize on immediate interest, as the data shows, allowing you to "strike while the iron is hot." Hopefully, you can see how powerful this can be when leveraged for your business.

Now, let's discuss where live webinars excel and where automation is most effective. There's a place for both. And as we just showed with regards to how people actually use webinars and how registrants and attendees actually show up to events, there are definitely times when automated webinars just make more sense for your business. But that's obviously not to say that an automated webinar is the right solution 100% of the time. Some other data points that we've been able to pull from our real-world analytics are that while automated webinars tend to get significantly higher attendance, live webinars can get higher engagement, can, on average, hold audience attention for longer periods of time (probably due to that higher engagement), and also generally just get more clicks to your offer (again, probably due to that higher engagement).

What does this mean for you? When should you choose a live event versus an automated event? Well, if you're struggling to choose between an automated or live event, and you know there's going to be a large number of attendees, due to live webinars typically holding audience attention better for longer periods of time, getting more engagement overall, and generally sending more eyeballs and clicks to your offers or sales pages, a live webinar is generally going to be the recommended choice in that situation. Plus, if you knock it out of the park on a live webinar, chat engagement is great, and you find yourself just firing on all cylinders that day, it's then super easy to take that live webinar recording and convert it into an automated webinar where it can then work for you, selling more on autopilot. So, that's a scenario where live webinars might be better. But on the flip side, if you have a busy schedule and you don't have the time or resources to be constantly running live webinars, then automated webinars are a godsend. And again, if you don't have a ton of traffic, automated webinars can also be perfect for that situation. This allows you to continuously collect the leads and registrants as they trickle into your funnel on your registration page, and then you can immediately view your content without them needing to wait for a time when you might actually be available to go live.

For example, if you're only able to have one live webinar session and it's weeks or even months away, someone visiting your registration page is liable to not even bother. But if they come to your registration page and your automated webinar is available to watch immediately or within a few minutes—as the data we showed clearly spells out—people are much more likely to actually attend your event once they register for it in that automated webinar case. So, with all that in mind, a lot of this still comes down to personal preference. Maybe you prefer automated webinars more like Phil does, or maybe you want to engage more with your audience live. That is a personal preference. But hopefully, with the data we just brought out for you, you'll feel empowered no matter whether you want to go down the fully live route or the automated route.

On that note, one type of automated webinar that has worked exceptionally well in my business is "just-in-time" webinars. As I've honed my skills with webinars over time, I've learned a great deal from running hundreds, if not thousands, of them. One of the key insights I've gained is an understanding of human nature when it comes to showing up for webinars.

We've already shared data on the differences between live and automated webinars, but on a more intuitive level, you start to notice that, especially with decreasing attention spans and busier schedules, having people attend a webinar at a specific time often results in lower attendance. This is also supported by some of the data we discussed earlier. One of the things we found particularly effective when we began running automated webinars was the concept of the just-in-time webinar. Essentially, this means that someone could come in and watch an automated event "just in time," meaning within 5 minutes, 10 minutes, 15 minutes, or even in some cases, 30 minutes into the future. Basically, they could watch the webinar on demand. And in doing so, they get the best of both worlds because it's showing up similarly to a live event, but it's happening right away.

They don't have to wait for a set time. You don't have to wait for 3 p.m. the same day or 2 p.m. the next day. Essentially, they could get the content that they need virtually instantly, but because it is still a time commitment, you do get the benefit of that first micro-commitment of someone taking that first step into the marketing funnel. So it works really, really well for that. We have experimented with different types of just-in-time webinars. We've learned that we really like the five-minute option because these days, even waiting 15 minutes is enough time for someone to lose their attention and go scroll off and do something else. Whereas a five-minute timer after someone joins a webinar is short enough that they will stick around and be able to watch the webinar right away, leading to much higher automated webinar attendance rates.

A bit more on how just-in-time webinars work: Imagine the scenario at the top of the hour. For example, if it's 12:00 p.m. and someone arrives at the landing page for your automated webinar at 12:01 p.m., and you're running a just-in-time webinar every five minutes, the next session will be at 12:05 p.m., starting in just 4 minutes. On the other hand, if you're running a 15-minute just-in-time webinar, the next session would be at 12:15 p.m., starting in 14 minutes.

Can you see the difference? If you were in the attendee's shoes, would you prefer to watch a webinar in the next 4 minutes or wait 14 minutes? Most likely, you'd choose the one starting in 4 minutes because, within 14 minutes, anything could happen—you might get distracted by another website, receive a phone call, or get a text message. Given today's short attention spans, holding someone's focus for long is incredibly challenging.

So that's the power of just-in-time webinars. And that actually segues into another really powerful option that we've learned, which is what's called "instant watch." A video sales letter is when someone puts their information onto a page and then watches a video on the next page. That's essentially a video sales letter funnel. And video sales letter funnels are great in the sense that people can watch the content right away, but they obviously have some flaws. When we were building WebinarKit, one of the things that we were thinking about is that it's awesome to have just-in-time webinars because, obviously, there's a function for those, and there's a benefit to those. Especially if someone could sign up in the next 5 minutes, you get that first micro-commitment from them. They feel like they signed up for something that's not just instant. They do have to wait a few minutes to get to that thing, which leads to higher attendance in that aspect. But at the same time, we know that there are many ways to do something. So, we wanted to experiment a bit with instant watches. And basically, what that means is, what if we could combine the power of a webinar watch room with the power of the instant accessibility of a video sales letter funnel? And that's essentially what the instant watch option is.

Basically, someone could sign up to watch the webinar instantly. They don't have to wait a minute. They don't have to wait four minutes. They don't have to wait 15 minutes. They just go into the webinar watch room right away. The difference between that and a video sales letter funnel is that with an automated webinar funnel, in addition to having the video playing, which is all it would be if it were on a static video sales letter page, you also have the power of webinars right there for someone to use such as engagement, polls, the live chat, the automated chat messages, the ability to email questions, of course, depending on what platform you're using, all of which these features are included inside of WebinarKit. That said, this is another powerful option for you to get out there to show people and give them that option.

We like to experiment with adding an instant watch and a five-minute just-in-time option to our webinar registration page. This means that when someone visits the webinar registration page, they will have a choice. Maybe some people want to grab the option to watch it right this second. Maybe some people do want to wait 5 minutes. In any case, you're appealing to both types of individuals by giving them both options. So, that's something that you can experiment with on your registration page.

Again, having access to all of these tools and how easy they are is just going to make it much easier for you to deploy them and be ahead of 99% of other marketers when it comes to getting results in your business.

Personal Case Studies

Back when I used to launch information products, I often started with automated live webinars, as I mentioned earlier. During the live webinars, I was incredibly nervous and dealt with many of the challenges we've discussed in this chapter. To maintain the structure of a set-time event, we eventually decided to take a recording of the webinar and run it at a specific time. During these sessions, we would still be present to answer chat questions and interact with attendees.

We'd announce a live webinar at, say, 7 p.m., and people would join at that exact time, with the recorded presentation playing while we answered their chat questions. This approach worked well overall. However, one challenge was maintaining the illusion of a fully live event, especially when we couldn't respond verbally. People would often ask, "Is this live?" and without being live on the audio, it was much harder to maintain that impression.

Then, at one point, we made a powerful discovery.

We realized that most of the engagement during a live webinar happens at the very beginning and the very end—when you're interacting with the audience and answering questions. This led us to think: *What if we created a special type of webinar where the beginning is live, allowing you to talk to attendees, address them by name, and respond directly to questions like, 'Is this live?' with a confident, 'Yes, John, this is live.'* Then, seamlessly transition to a pre-recorded segment for the bulk of the content, and finally, transition back to live interaction for the Q&A at the end.

We began experimenting with this approach in our business, which has proven to be incredibly powerful. It allowed us to leverage the personalization of the live introduction, where we could call out attendees by name—a highly effective tactic—and engage with them directly. At the same time, we don't have to repeatedly deliver the same middle portion of the presentation. This approach is what we call the "hybrid live automated webinar."

This hybrid model is part live, part automated, but mostly automated. It saves you from having to present the bulk of the content repeatedly while still providing a live experience at the beginning and end. This method is particularly effective if you plan to run the same presentation regularly, such as weekly.

So, in summary, we've now covered live webinars, where you have a specific date and time for the event and fully automated webinars. The hybrid live webinar combines the best of both worlds, offering a powerful tool for your business without requiring you to do the majority of the work every time.

We've covered just-in-time webinars, which are automated webinars that could be anywhere from 5 to 15 to 30 minutes in the future when someone visits the registration page. We've covered instant watch, which combines the power of a video sales letter funnel with the power of a webinar watch room, allowing people to go directly into the webinar. And now we've even covered the hybrid live automated webinar, where you could take a webinar recording and simply do the intro, which introduces people, and then the frequently asked questions at the end live. This gives you so much power in your business. Again, these are all things that we essentially have built into WebinarKit so that you could just tick a box and get each of these settings done for you incredibly easily.

You might be asking yourself, *If I am doing a fully automated webinar, how do I get the frequently asked questions?* Because at the end of the webinar are questions, right? So how do you get the frequently asked questions if it's an automated webinar? So there are a few ways to do this.

One of the ways is if you are doing the first few webinars live, you're going to see in the chat box, what are all of the questions that people are asking.

You could actually just compile a list of every single question that people asked. A tool like WebinarKit lets you review your chat libraries anyway, and you can easily compile a list of those questions, or you could do it manually. Essentially, you can take all of that information and then just answer those questions in a webinar recording. So that's one way to do it. Suppose you don't want to do a live webinar at all. In that case, you can go back to what we talked about in one of the previous chapters and go to a tool like Claude.ai, which already knows your customer avatar, and ask it, "What would be the top 15 frequently asked questions people would ask for this avatar and this product and service on this webinar?" Then, you could take those 15 questions and put them into a frequently asked question on the recording. So, these are some really powerful options for you to use in your business when it comes to automating webinars. If you were worried that automated webinars had limits, hopefully, this chapter shows you just how easy they could be and all of the powerful options at your disposal that you could use to deploy into your business to increase your profits.

A quick note about saving chat messages to display them during replays or your webinars later. As we've discussed a few times during this chapter, chat simulation can be a huge part of automated webinars that can really help in a variety of ways. For example, using a real chat history log, set up your automated webinar "replay" that shows all of the chat message engagement that you had from a real live event or series of live events. This can be a super effective strategy to leverage your live sessions and convert them to an automated session while still bringing some of that live energy to your automated webinar attendees ethically and honestly. But then you might wonder, *Wait a second, do I have to manually save and store and look up all these chat messages that people leave in my chat and look up all the good ones and kind of filter them out and then manually paste them into my automated webinar later?* That could take ages to get fully set up. But again, any self-respecting modern webinar platform is going to be able to save the day here again. And with a powerful webinar platform, like WebinarKit, for example, it's so easy to import real chat history messages into your automated webinar chat simulator. As long as you pick the right tool, it literally just takes seconds to import either individual messages or even an entire webinar's chat history directly into your automated webinar or webinars so that you can leverage that real-life human engagement that you've previously gotten, and that can really supercharge your automated webinars. This is a powerful tool to have at your disposal, and again, with the right tool like WebinarKit, it's super easy to do.

Don't forget to check out our full suite of gifts—marketing resources and more—to help you jumpstart your sales with webinars in record time:

or go to https://getwebinarkit.com/book-resources

CHAPTER 7

How to Use Organic and Paid Marketing Strategies to Drive Targeted Traffic to Your Webinars Every Day

Have you ever wondered, *Okay, I have a webinar now, but how the heck am I going to get people to actually watch it?*

I'll let you in on a little secret: It's much easier than you think. Getting traffic is not hard. When I started an online business, one of the things I constantly worried about was, *How am I going to get traffic?*

You may be thinking this at some point in your business as well. How am I going to get enough eyeballs to view my content? I remember thinking to myself, anyone can make a sales page, anyone can make a webinar, but not everyone knows how to drive traffic. As I became more advanced in marketing, I learned that my perception wasn't entirely accurate. Traffic is obviously very important, but at the end of the day, it's actually much more about getting the right message in front of the right person.

If you can get the right message in front of the right person over and over again, you're going to make more sales. That's where traffic comes in, but the bulk of the effort actually needs to be on getting those other parts right first. You could have the worst sales page in the world and drive a million visitors to it, but that sales page isn't going to convert a single one of them if it's terrible.

Conversely, you could have the best sales page in the world—absolutely amazing—and if you drive only five people to it, maybe you convert two of them, and maybe they tell their friends. So, at the end of the day, the product and the marketing around the product matter much more than the traffic. That was a big perception change for me throughout my online business journey.

That said, as you know, the majority of this book has focused on the importance of getting your webinar funnel correct. Thankfully, you made the smart move of picking up this book, so you've learned just how easy it is to build the right marketing funnel using webinars. This means that you can have minimal amounts of traffic and still convert a significant number of people, using the power of AI to do it in record time. Remember, we provide all the resources you need, which are linked inside this book.

When I used to run traffic on Pinterest, it was all about driving tons of volume because, back then, it was very easy to get traffic from Pinterest. You could drive over 100,000 visitors per month from Pinterest for free.

However, when I was driving that traffic, I was sending it to a blog that wasn't optimized for conversions. It didn't really build a relationship with anyone, and a lot of the traffic I was getting wasn't necessarily my ideal customer avatar. It was people who generally liked the subject, but they weren't pre-vetted through the kind of deep customer avatar understanding we achieve using AI, as discussed in previous chapters. So, I quickly realized that it isn't necessarily about the quantity of traffic but about having the right product and driving the right people to that funnel.

I really want to make sure that you understand this concept before we move forward: You don't need a lot of traffic if you have the right funnel.

And thankfully, since you're taking action by reading this book and seeing how easy it is to set up the right webinar funnel, you won't need a lot of traffic. If we just do some basic math, we know that webinars convert much higher than static sales pages. For example, someone who visits a sales page, as we've discussed, isn't building the same level of relationship as they would through a webinar, which is much more intimate and dives deeper into the *why* behind someone's interest. You're going to be able to convert a much higher percentage of those people.

For example, 100 people visiting a website or a sales page is very different from getting 100 people to register for your webinar funnel. One hundred people registering for your webinar funnel could potentially result in five sales, depending on the price point. One hundred people visiting your website, especially if you're selling something for $1,000 or more, might not yield any sales, and in most cases, it would take a much larger amount of targeted traffic to start generating sales. So you should be feeling pretty excited. Why?

Because I just told you that you don't need that many people coming to your webinar funnel to generate significant sales. That's exciting because it means you've already done the right setup, so you don't need a lot of people.

When it comes to driving traffic, you might be asking yourself, *Do I need to start with paid ads? I'm scared of burning a hole in my wallet with paid ads.* While paid ads work, and we're going to give you strategies on how to use them in this book, I want to let you know that you don't even need to start with paid ads.

A few years ago, when I was running a webinar coaching boot camp, I taught a concept called the "family and friends webinar." The idea came from my experience selling knives for a company when I was 19 years old. During sales training, they told me to make a huge list of every single person I knew who had a kitchen. I remember making that list and realizing that I knew a lot more people than I initially thought. I realized that this concept could be applied to getting people to your webinar. Why not start with your network? At the end of the day, as much as you might think you don't have a network to start with, you actually do. Everyone has some sort of network—it could be your Facebook friends, work colleagues, a few people on LinkedIn, or the 20 people you've built up over the past few years through various events, friends of friends, or acquaintances. These are all part of your initial network: your "family and friends network."

I instructed people to start inviting everyone they knew to attend when they were ready to run their first webinar. One of my clients, who was going to teach people about an elopement business, did just that. He posted to his Facebook profile and LinkedIn, shared it by email with a few people he knew, and even sent it through text messages. He had about 15 people show up to his first webinar. Over the course of the next week, he closed two of those 15 people into his high-ticket program. He was amazed at how easy it was to see results with a small audience.

Now, imagine if he had simply created a sales page and posted to the same number of people, saying, "Hey, check it out. I've got this thing for thousands of dollars; go visit this website." Do you think it would have had nearly the same effect? Absolutely not.

So, the concept of the family and friends webinar is one of the best places to start when looking for traffic to your webinar. Leverage your existing network, and from there, we'll teach you how to grow your existing network so you always have a bigger audience for growing your business.

The first traffic strategy I'd like to cover is building your audience. This is a concept that, if you understand and apply it alongside high-converting webinars, will ensure you never struggle to sell anything again in your life. Because when it comes down to it, a bigger audience means more of the right customer avatars at your fingertips when you need traffic. Building an audience can take many forms—it could be having a larger group of Facebook friends, more connections on LinkedIn, or growing your email list.

One of the most important pieces of advice I received when I started online in 2013 was: You own your list of names, phone numbers, emails, and addresses. You do not own Facebook, LinkedIn, or Instagram. These platforms can sweep the rug out from under you at any time and take away all the audiences you've built on them.

So, while having a Facebook group, an Instagram following, or a lot of friends on Facebook and LinkedIn is great, remember that you don't own that data. You definitely want to make sure you're building an email list at least, and consider building a list of phone numbers for people who engage with your content and take action with you.

One of the easiest ways to do this is by inviting your audiences to sign up for your webinar. When you do this, you'll start building your email list (and your phone number list if you choose that option), something that is easily done using WebinarKit or similar software. You'll be building an audience for the long term.

Now, don't discount the power of building even a small audience. This is something that will propel your business forever. If you can understand the concept of consistently building your audience, even slowly, and consistently getting some sort of marketing message in front of them, you will consistently generate more sales for your business. This was a concept that took me many years to fully grasp because, especially coming from the world of direct response marketing, we were regularly taught to maximize immediate sales.

But what's ultimately going to build abundance in your business, whether it's this business or any business you start in the future, is building up the right systems to have consistent sales over time. The concept of building up your own network and audience and getting your marketing message in front of them consistently will do just that.

When I was a child, I would regularly look up at signs for Pepsi or Coke and wonder to myself, *Everyone already knows what Pepsi or Coke is—why do they keep advertising?* As I started understanding online business better, I realized that you need to stay top of mind and relevant. Tons of other businesses are competing for the attention of your customer avatar at all times, and at a minimum, you need to be in the competition. If you are not seen, you are not heard—you're simply not in the conversation, and you won't have people remember you or buy from you, no matter how prominent your brand might be at this time.

So, understanding that concept, how do you actually start building your own audience? Two of the things I immediately started doing for myself, and that I recommend you do as well, are building your Facebook and LinkedIn audiences. This is extremely low-hanging fruit. Again, we don't want to rely entirely on these platforms for all of our traffic, but they are excellent starting points to build a pipeline of people that you can then drive to your automated or live webinars, ultimately building your own email and phone number list.

LinkedIn and Facebook allow you to go in and simply friend a certain number of people every day. How does that work? You can do it in a few ways, but the easiest is to find Facebook groups that discuss a certain topic. For example, if you're in the dog niche, join groups for dog lovers or dog owners. From there, look for the people who are actively engaging in the chat, such as those asking a lot of questions. These are the people who are engaged and more likely to be buyers. Start friending these people.

Before you do that, though, it's best to have a bit of information about your business on your Facebook profile. Your profile should at least explain what you do and potentially feature a banner image, as well as a few recent posts linked to your Facebook group (which we'll talk about in a minute) or, at a minimum, inviting people to your webinars or sharing some authority content on a relevant topic. Hint: You can use AI to create authority content. In previous chapters, we discussed how you can use Claude and other tools to easily generate content for your webinar. Use the same tool to ask for five valuable pieces of information to share on your Facebook as authority content targeting your ideal customer avatar. Post those to your Facebook and then start the friend request method. Friend 30 to 50 people every day within your niche.

Over time, you'll build a network of thousands of people who are your ideal target audience. Now, when you post on Facebook to invite them to a webinar, what do you think will happen? You'll get amazing results.

One of the best ways to post that leads to the most registrants and engagement is to frame it as an inquiry rather than an announcement. Instead of saying, "Hey, I'm running a webinar this week; click this link to sign up," say, "I'm getting a lot of interest in running a webinar about [XYZ]. I'll cover [X, Y, and Z]. Would you be interested in this?" You could frame it as a free webinar and add, "So I'm looking to start a free webinar on [XYZ]. Is this something you'd be interested in?" You can also use Claude to craft this post as well.

What will happen is you'll start getting a lot of people commenting below: "Hey, I'm interested," "Hey, I'm in," "Sounds great!" Over time, those are the people you can engage with. You can now choose to post the webinar registration link directly in the comments or message them privately with the link. By doing it privately, you're also building a more direct connection, which could lead to a sale.

This sounds super easy, right? Anyone can do this. So when you think it's hard to get traffic, just remember that if you can get 30 or 50 people engaging on a post like this once a month or once a week for a webinar, how much could your business change? One of my clients only had 15 people show up to his first webinar and made two sales worth thousands of dollars.

LinkedIn works similarly to Facebook. It's super easy to get traffic. Simply go to LinkedIn, search for people within your niche (for example, coaches if that's your target), and follow 20 or 30 people a day, depending on LinkedIn's current limit. By doing this, you're growing your network for free. These are two strategies anyone can implement right now, and it only takes a few minutes each day to start building your network. How big could your network be in three months? How big could it be in one month?

Is it big enough to get a few people on a webinar and convert a couple of them every week into high-ticket customers? Right there, you have the foundations to create a six-figure business and potentially scale to seven figures. If you can grasp the concept of building an audience consistently and regularly putting that webinar in front of them in an automated fashion, you're well on your way to transforming your business.

Now, that's the concept of building your own audience, but there's another powerful strategy I've used for years and still use in my business to reach more people. It's called OPA, which stands for "Other People's Audiences." What if you didn't even have to build your own audience? What if you could leverage the hard work someone else put into building theirs? That's where the OPA strategy comes in. Essentially, you create a referral program for your product or service and then approach others with established audiences, saying, "Hey, I'd like to demonstrate what my product or service does on a free webinar for your audience. I'll give you a commission for any sales made from your audience."

When I was selling courses a few years ago, this strategy was extremely effective for me. Every week, I'd find someone willing to promote my webinar to their audience, and every week, sales would come in from leveraging other people's audiences.

There are a few ways to connect with these individuals, but having your own audience can be helpful because they may want access to your audience in exchange for access to theirs. This is called a webinar swap, where you promote their webinar to your audience, and they promote yours to theirs. It's simple, powerful, and often, in addition to this, you can find people willing to let you run your webinar to their audience because the commissions are enticing, and they need to make money.

These strategies illustrate that the majority of benefits come from simply having a webinar funnel and building one. Between the technology we've discussed and the use of AI (and your smart decision to read this book), it's incredibly easy and fast to set up a webinar funnel that can transform your business. From there, driving traffic isn't particularly hard.

Using TikTok Videos

Colton Havens uses organic, short-form videos to get traffic to his webinars on WebinarKit. We asked him to share this—it's so easy, you can do the same thing:

"I'm going to show you how I get people to my WebinarKit webinar using TikTok videos. The best part about these videos is they're non-talking heads. You don't have to speak, and they're very, very simple to make. If you can take a selfie video, you can create the video yourself. You can create it right inside TikTok's 'create video' function or just use the video option on your phone. I'm going to make it in 15 seconds. And I'm just going to kind of put some space here and point and smile for 7 seconds."

Now, we're going to add some simple text to the video. Free video editing applications on your phone like Capcut can do this, or you can do the editing right inside TikTok or on Instagram Reels for simplicity. I'm adding the following text, and it comes out looking like this:

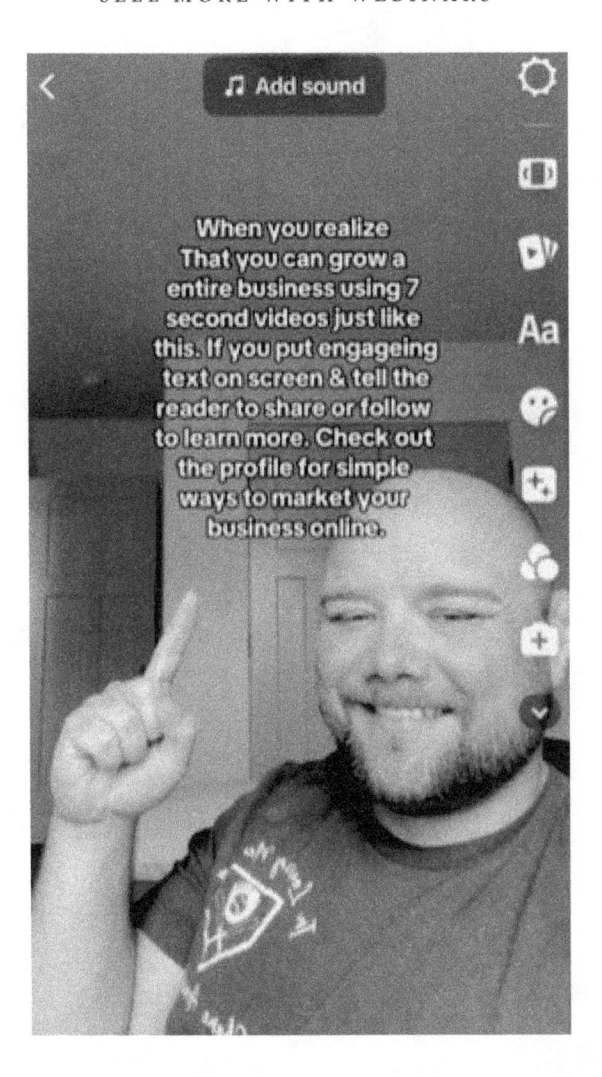

From there, you add a sound and post it across TikTok, Instagram Reels, Facebook Reels, and YouTube Shorts.

From there, do this daily for best results or as often as possible. Try different hooks around your ideal client or customer's pain points; you can even use AI to come up with new hooks. Reshare your best-performing videos.

Do this, and you can get easy, consistent traffic. It works great for automated webinars or even weekly live ones!

In addition to this, because you grabbed this book, we have some traffic resources that we've also included for you to get started driving traffic very easily to your webinars, which are included in our resources linked throughout this book. included in our resources linked throughout this book.

Scan the QR code:

or go to https://getwebinarkit.com/book-resources

CHAPTER 8

The Little-Known Webinar Formats That Can Increase Your Profit Potential Over 5x

Once your webinar is up and running, these strategies can help you truly take things to the next level. The goal of webinars is to get started. One of the biggest issues I've noticed is people's mindset when it comes to business—they feel overwhelmed and get stuck in analysis paralysis, and I don't want that to happen to you. So, make sure you don't jump to this chapter until you've completed everything in the previous ones. Fortunately, we've made it as easy as possible for you.

You already know the power of the customer avatar. You already know the power of today's AI, which can get most of the marketing content done for you very quickly. You have all the resources to set up a webinar presentation in record time by following our format.

You can also use tools like WebinarKit to build the funnel in as little as ten minutes without needing any technical skills. Obviously, that's the first place to start because simply getting out there and running your first webinar is where the main results will come from. That said, once you've got things rocking and rolling, we'd like to share some powerful strategies that took us years to learn—strategies that can help you really reach the next level. Again, these are not required to get results, so there's no need to start with them, but they can give you a powerful edge, putting you in the top 1% of webinar marketers.

One of the biggest secrets I've learned in business comes down to consistency. I've talked about this in previous chapters, but the concept of more touchpoints and more consistency in your business is where most of the results will come from. With the help of AI, it's easier than ever to have the right messaging dialed in, as we've discussed. Once you've got this down, you simply need to get that message in front of more people more consistently. That's it—that's the secret. That's all you need to do in business.

So, how do you actually do that? One of the things that works extremely well is having a weekly webinar newsletter. What does this mean? Well, it can take many different forms.

One way to do a newsletter is to present a different webinar topic to your audience every week while selling the same product. Another way is to take the same webinar and change the headline to appeal to a different subgroup on your list. You can also use AI to come up with ten different headlines for the same webinar. Each week, change the headline, do the intro, and end live using a hybrid format like we taught in the previous chapter, and keep the main content of the webinar the same. What's really interesting is how many people might attend the same webinar three times but only buy on the third time because the headline completely changed how they view the content of the webinar. This is the power of letting people see things through a different headline or lens, and that's what you're tapping into with this strategy.

When running a weekly webinar newsletter, another powerful strategy is to use the "other people's audiences" strategy we discussed earlier. What if you could get a few partners to come on your webinar show every week? That way, instead of promoting the same content over and over again, you can promote someone else's product based on their webinar to your audience each week. In turn, they will promote your webinar to their audience. Now you're making double the amount of money—you're promoting their webinar to your audience, providing fresh content every week that makes you money without requiring you to constantly come up with new content, and you're also getting your product sold to a new audience every week via someone else's audience. This is a really powerful strategy.

In addition to this, one of the things that works extremely well is turning your one-day webinar into a multi-day event. On that note, I want to share something we've touched on throughout the book but really want to dive into more deeply—something that, if you understand it, will unlock maximum results in your business. This is the concept of the power of touchpoint marketing.

Years ago, there was a concept in Hollywood called the "Rule of Seven." Hollywood executives believed that people needed to see details about a movie seven times before they became excited enough to go see it. These days, seven might be on the lower end because, as we mentioned earlier, attention spans are much shorter. The goal now is to get in front of people many more times than seven, which is why we emphasize increasing touchpoints much more quickly and easily.

One way to quickly rack up touchpoints is by turning your one-day webinar into a multi-day webinar. What does this mean? We talked about the four components of a successful webinar, the objection crushers, and then the offer. What if you took each of these concepts and broke them up into separate days?

Instead of creating one touchpoint, you have now created four. Spending time with someone is a major factor in liking, knowing, and trusting them, according to numerous studies.

In the 1960s, Robert Zajonc conducted the first research on the psychological phenomenon known as the Mere Exposure Effect. His studies discovered that people frequently favor things just because they are accustomed to them. This effect is also true for people; being around someone more often can make you like and trust them more.

In 1976, British psychologists Short, Williams, and Christie created the Social Presence Theory, which posits that a communication medium can foster greater intimacy and trust the more "social presence" it permits. When it comes to online communication, webinars offer a higher degree of social presence due to their interactive features and video.

Gefen and Straub (2003), researchers and professors, discovered that increased social presence in communication (such as live interaction in webinars and video) can result in higher levels of trust in e-commerce settings.

Let's look at a straightforward scenario. Suppose that for a month, you and your friends went to a party every Friday. You meet someone and greet them for two minutes on the first Friday. You see them again a week later, and you have a five-minute conversation. By the third party, you have seen them more frequently and, despite the fact that you do not really know them, you begin to feel more at ease with their appearance, personality, and vibe. You will feel much more at ease approaching the fourth party because you will almost feel like you know them.

The time commitment needed to establish varying degrees of friendships was the subject of an important study by Jeffrey Hall, a professor of communication studies at the University of Kansas. He discovered that 50 hours is the bare minimum of time required to qualify someone as a casual friend. Likewise, it takes 80 to 100 hours for regular friends. It takes around 200 hours on average to develop a close friendship.

What is this telling you? Using the example of the person you see at a party, it explains that the more time and consistency you spend with someone, the closer you will find your relationship with them. Given that we have discussed webinars as a means of fostering a closer relationship, the four-day event seems like a perfect fit, does not it? If you split the same webinar into four days, that person will become accustomed to seeing and hearing you every day for four or five days, which will increase their captive time and help them develop a stronger relationship with you.

It's really twofold: They get more time with you overall, building that know, like, and trust factor, and you're also training them to see your face every day and whatever awesome vibe you're bringing to the webinar or challenge. So, when the five days are up, they're thinking, *I don't really want this to end. I want this to continue,* and the next logical step is for them to take action with you.

You might be asking yourself, *Is it hard to transition my one-day webinar into a four-day or five-day event?* It actually couldn't be easier. You guessed it—use AI to take that one-day webinar and transform it into a four- or five-day event.

Tools like WebinarKit, which we built to include four- or five-day virtual event functionality (or three-day, or whatever you'd like), make it very easy to create an event where people can engage with you every day for a set number of days. Now, you're combining the main concept—consistency and touchpoint marketing, based on proven studies—with the technology and power of webinar marketing to get the best of both worlds and produce a slew of sales in your business.

Multi-day events are a powerful way to move people through or rearrange your content in a way that leverages multiple angles, keeps your audience engaged, and constantly provides different touchpoints with them. This keeps them focused on your message or branding, connects you with your audience more and more, and ultimately hits them at various angles and touchpoints, which is great for your sales and conversions.

But what does this look like in practice? It's really not hard at all. Once you have your basic webinar content set up, it's super easy to break that content into several sections that can be used across various days or webinars in your multi-day event. There's no need to overthink this part—it's really that simple.

Anyone can do this. For example, if you have a 90-minute webinar presentation, as we showed you earlier in this book, you can easily split it into, say, a five-day challenge, with each day's content being 15 to 20 minutes long. This is a great way to increase engagement and to speak to different people who might resonate more with a five-day challenge. Maybe they don't want to sit through a 90-minute to two-hour (or longer) webinar presentation, but a few minutes every day might be more their style. By the end of that five-day challenge, your attendees will be ready to move on to whatever the next step is in your funnel—whether that's booking a call with you, purchasing your product, or signing up for your coaching program.

Of course, picking the right tool is crucial here because not all platforms are made equal when it comes to running your multi-day events. WebinarKit makes it super easy to take your split-up content and convert it into a series of webinars. For example, you could set up your five-day challenge in software like WebinarKit in literally just minutes. So, be sure to pick the right platform that allows you to set up your multi-day content easily and also, crucially, allows your registrants and attendees to view your multi-day events and content easily. In other words, you don't want your attendees to have to re-register for every day of your challenge. That's just a pain for them. A good tool or software will let your registrants register for your multi-day event or challenge once, and they'll automatically be able to join each day.

Their link will automatically take them to the right session, and they'll get reminder emails for each session in your series in your multi-day event setup. This is super important.

The Challenge Webinars

Rocio Arroyave, also referred to as "The Challenge Queen," is a dynamic entrepreneur whose 5-Day Challenge Framework has revolutionized online marketing. We will now also discuss a case study of her.

To demonstrate the strength of challenges and even offer some advice from one of the greatest, we asked her to share a brief excerpt:

Three to five-day challenge webinars are a powerful tool that have significantly improved our business and the businesses of our clients. One of the most significant changes has been the sharp rise in conversion rates, particularly for expensive products.

Challenge webinars frequently attain conversion rates of 10%–20% or higher, whereas traditional webinars may see conversion rates of 2%–8% (particularly with cold traffic, also known as Paid Ads).

In his $2,500/month TikTok Agency DFY Service, Colton Havens, CEO of HYPE Productions, saw a 20% conversion rate after introducing a challenge webinar called the "$100K View Challenge," in which he taught people how to get over 100,000 views on their short-form videos. Due to increased capacity and demand, he raised his prices as a result of his success.

Important Elements of a Successful Challenge:

- **Live sessions every day.** Present the key points, respond to inquiries, and interact with participants in real time.
- **Actionable tasks.** Encourage students to apply the concepts they have learned to their everyday tasks.
- **Community involvement.** Facilitate communication and support within a specific area, usually a Facebook group.
- **Progressively solving issues.** Deal with a problem in a different way every day.
- **Final offer.** Present your offering as the logical next step.

Differences from Conventional Webinars:

- **Extended participation.** Develops stronger bonds over several days.
- **Comprehensive handling of objections.** Plenty of time to address different objections.
- **Progressive learning.** Improved information application and retention.
- **Community development.** Promotes collaboration and brotherhood.
- **Greater ability to convert.** More time to prove value and earn trust.
- **Repurposed content.** Utilize produced content in upcoming promotions.

Psychological concepts:

- **Consistency and commitment.** Increased dedication from participants over days.

- **Social evidence.** Wins and progress together increase credibility.
- **Mutual support.** Multi-day value provision encourages responsibility.
- **Urgency and scarcity.** Limited deals encourage choices.

Other advantages:

- **Deeper comprehension** of client needs, stronger relationships with participants, and increased trust.
- **Social proof** and useful content for later use.
- **Quick expansion of an email list** with the potential to go viral.
- **Scalable business plan** with tiers of offerings and evergreen potential.
- **Economic benefits** include lower marketing expenses, more revenue per customer, and recurring income.

Your challenge webinar will effectively educate, engage, and convert if you make use of these components.

How to Host a Webinar Challenge:

1. **Break down the information.** Determine the main ideas and information pertaining to the group.
2. **Daily framework:**
   a. **Day 1:** Introduction and Instruction on Handling Product or Program Objections (also called Vehicle Objections)
      i. Talk about your story and background.
      ii. Explain the basic idea or approach.
      iii. Address any skepticism regarding the viability of your strategy.

b. **Day 2:** Instruction on Handling Abilities Objections (also called Internal Objections)
   i. Concentrate on the self-doubts of participants.
   ii. Offer exercises to build trust.
   iii. Talk about the achievements of people who have surmounted comparable challenges.
c. **Day 3:** Instruction on Handling External Objections (also called Circumstances Objections)
   i. Address issues pertaining to time, resources, or assistance.
   ii. Provide answers for typical external obstacles.
   iii. Show how your approach performs under different conditions.
d. **Day 4: Handling Another Complaint and Making Your Offer**
   i. Prior to presenting your offer, address another issue they might be considering that is critically important to resolve.
   ii. Review the value that was offered in the days prior.
   iii. Present your service or product as the logical next step.
   iv. Emphasize your offer's special advantages.
e. **Day 5: Handle Another Complaint, Summarize, and Re-Sell Your Offer**
   i. On the final day, the lesson ought to be less demanding than on earlier days.
   ii. List the main conclusions drawn from the challenge.
   iii. Address all remaining objections.
   iv. Create a sense of urgency for action by restating your offer.

During the Challenge Tips:

- **Add interactive elements.** Incorporate surveys, tests, and live Q&A sessions to maintain participants' interest.
- **Create supporting resources.** To assist participants in putting the lessons into practice, provide workbooks, cheat sheets, and templates.
- **Configure your technology stack.** Make sure all required technology is prepared and tested, including community platforms, email automation tools, and webinar software.
- **Develop a plan for promotion.** Develop a thorough strategy to advertise the challenge via email marketing, social media, and collaborations in order to increase sign-ups.
- **Get ready for live delivery.** Practice your presentations, make sure all the materials are prepared, and prepare a contingency plan in case of technical difficulties.
- **Prepare for a follow-up.** To keep people interested and get feedback, create a follow-up email sequence for both buyers and non-buyers and plan post-challenge touchpoints.

These steps will help you turn your conventional webinar into an interesting challenge webinar with a high conversion rate that consistently delivers value and carefully guides participants to your offer.

Following the Challenge:

- Sequence of follow-up emails for both buyers and non-buyers.
- Send offers to buyers.
- Collect input for future enhancements.

Selecting the length of the challenge:

According to Rocio, "I have found that 4- or 5-day challenges are the best for turning cold leads into buyers for expensive offers." Deeper connection and more thorough objection handling are made possible by the longer time. However, I have found that 3-day challenges are very effective and easier to fill for simpler offers or when I am testing new markets. The challenge length should be matched to the demands of your audience and your particular offer.

Keep in mind that there isn't a universal solution. The audience, objectives, and particular circumstances of your company will determine the optimal challenge duration. Try out various durations to see what suits you best; do not be scared to try them.

By addressing objections, delivering consistent value, and guiding participants toward your offer, you can turn your conventional webinar into an interesting, high-converting challenge webinar.

Finally, I am thrilled to present to you an exclusive present: the Challenger's Toolkit, which is powered by AI. This book is available to readers at SecretDoor.TheChallengeQueen.com. This set of tools includes:

- The Challenger's Playbook.
- AI-Powered Impact Offer Builder & Target Audience Analyzer.
- Exclusive AI Builder for the five-day challenge.

By using AI to analyze your audience, create compelling offers, and create captivating 5-day challenges, these tools will assist you in creating high-converting challenges. To get your free toolkit and improve the way you create challenges, go to SecretDoor.TheChallengeQueen.com right now. Challenge building's future is here—it is simple, efficient, and cost-free!

You can also set up your challenges on WebinarKit.com to be either live or automated. Start by visiting getwebinarkit.com.

So, how about using AI to turn your webinar into a challenge funnel like this? What if, despite the most recent developments in AI, you still find it a bit overwhelming to turn your webinar content into a multi-day event? If so, you can have the content and structure of your multi-day event planned out for you in a matter of seconds. Just visit Claude AI, ChatGPT, or your favorite AI chat tool and request that they divide your webinar presentation into a multi-day event. After copying and pasting your webinar presentation outline or even the entire content into the AI tool, you should be ready to go. It's truly that simple.

From there, you can make any tweaks or adjustments you feel might be necessary, but the AI has done the "hard work" for you.

Now that we've covered all the different ways you can take your main webinar content and get even better results with it, a few other things are worth mentioning. There's something called the five-day challenge or three-day challenge, which Rocio covers a bit above. That's one style. Another option is to simply do a three-day webinar series or workshop series. Whether you want to do three days or five days is totally up to you. These days, we believe four days is considered the perfect amount of time, but we always recommend experimenting.

Another powerful approach is running something called a "town hall." This is just a day where you invite all the webinar registrants you've built and say, "Hey, we're doing a live town hall." This is another powerful way to add a touchpoint to your business. You invite people to a town hall, where you can build a stronger relationship with all the people who have been following you, remind them of your product or service at the end, but do so in a more informal way that makes it feel like you're just trying to connect with them.

Often, people who are warm potential buyers appreciate when you show them your personal side, and that can be enough to push them over the edge to buy. You could run a one-day town hall to do this. During the town hall, you can also reinforce key concepts that lead them to conclude that your product or service is the best fit for them, but without a hard sell. Simply remind them it's available, then enjoy the town hall being your happy, merry self, and that can lead to more sales.

Another strategy that works well is running a virtual summit. You might be able to get webinar presentations from other people and do a two-day summit, for example, where you share four speakers per day for two days. This covers a variety of information, engages people very quickly, and can lead to a high influx of sales and trust in a short amount of time without even having to create most of the content yourself.

Another approach is to experiment with the wording of webinars. For example, calling a webinar a webinar—calling it a workshop, a challenge, a summit, a town hall, or a series. I've even seen people use the terms "mini-workshop" or "mini-webinar." You can experiment with these terms, too, and often, they're the same length as a regular webinar. Because, really, at the end of the day, sometimes changing the wording of what you're doing can be incredibly powerful in changing your audience's perspective and getting them to show up.

CHAPTER 9

Simple Webinar Extensions You Can Quickly Make to Unlock Long-Term Profits and Beat Your Competitors

As with anything, when you combine different strategies, you can achieve even better results. What do I mean by this? Webinars by themselves are incredibly powerful, as you've seen throughout this book, and they've been a tremendous benefit to my business. In Chapter 7, we discussed ways to take what's already working well and make it even better. This chapter will introduce even more strategies you can apply to your business to elevate your current success to the next level. By purchasing this book, you're gaining access to some of the most advanced concepts used by top-tier marketers. We're excited to share these insights with you—lessons we've learned from years of experience.

First, I want to share that in my experience as a direct response marketer, everything revolves around getting the sale now. Immediate sales are crucial, and webinars are designed to maximize both immediate and future buyers. That said, webinars also help build your long-term brand, creating a narrative around you and your product or service that keeps people engaged. They want to keep following your content and are more likely to buy your products because they feel connected to you. This is where the power of branding comes in.

When I started my online journey, I was focused on getting immediate sales. I didn't want to wait forever for results. However, as I've gained more experience, I've learned that the real key is to focus on both capturing immediate sales and building your brand for future sales. Understanding this concept—that it's not just about getting sales on a webinar but also about the power of branding—can lead to amazing results.

Let me share an anecdote from our business that might resonate with you. When we started selling WebinarKit through ads, we saw lots of sales. However, over time, we noticed that while our sales continued, many were not being attributed to Facebook ads. Initially, we thought this was due to tracking issues related to privacy and Apple OS updates. We tried different tracking software, but they didn't solve the problem. What we eventually discovered was that people were seeing our ads on Facebook and then Googling our brand rather than clicking the ad directly.

And then I thought about it for a second. Have you ever done this? Have you ever been on Facebook and seen an ad for something, but you didn't click the ad? But then, either immediately or a bit later, you remember what the ad said and what the brand or the person behind the ad was, and you go and Google it. Well, basically, this is what we learned was happening. Our ads were presenting a ton of brand awareness for people, but they weren't necessarily clicking those ads to take an immediate response. They now knew that we had a brand, and they either immediately or later went to Google to see what people were saying about our brand. And this is when we saw the power of building that brand. Now, one thing that I've seen a lot of webinar marketers do that I've never really understood and always disagreed with was focusing entirely on direct response conversions. This means that a lot of these marketers don't have a website for their product or service, or they might not even have a website for their own coaching brand, for their own selves.

And I always thought this was such a missed opportunity because, remember, when people see an ad for you, it's only natural that they wonder, *Is this person legit, or is this product legit?* And in this day and age, our society believes that when we Google something, there is a higher level of legitimacy if things pop up on Google that are positive. So, for example, if you are running ads for your webinar and you are a personal brand, how about having an optimized website that ranks at the top of Google? How about being on a few podcasts that rank at the top of Google and show you as an expert in your field? How about having your product or service ranked at the top of Google? And if this sounds silly to you, I am consistently shocked at how many top-tier, personal brand webinar marketers or even those pushing products don't have these simple things optimized.

It's literally, I would say, at this point, a huge credit to the fact that we still make money from ads. I've been in rooms with very advanced marketers who have looked at me and said, "Why are your ads doing so well? I don't actually understand it." And I will say to them, "I would say because it's less about the ad and more about the customer journey."

We understand that the ad simply gets the awareness about our brand out there these days. People are then going to Google us. So, if you haven't simply done a quick Google search over your name or over your product or service to go take a look at what it looks like, this is something that you can easily do to immediately increase the response that you get from your webinar product or service.

If you're running ads for a webinar under a personal brand and someone Googles you but finds nothing, their trust in you will be low, making them less likely to sign up. However, if they Google you and discover that you're active—perhaps they see you've been featured on multiple podcasts or have an impressive website showcasing your expertise and connections—they're far more likely to think, "Wow, this person is really accomplished."

Being on a webinar with someone like that is much more appealing, which will naturally increase the number of sign-ups. This means more people will attend your webinar at a lower cost, and more will engage. By doing this, you've effectively pre-framed yourself, your product, or your service from a higher level, leading to a higher number of sales.

And this has definitely been one of the secrets that's allowed us to see really good results running ads directly to our product or service and also to the webinars that sell our product or service. So, the first place to start is the power of branding. Additionally, imagine if there were a website where you ranked highly with excellent reviews for yourself, your product, or your service—perhaps a testimonials page that ranks well or a third-party site like G2 or Trustpilot with glowing reviews. These factors can significantly improve the results of your direct response efforts because people will Google you. If you're nowhere to be found, you're hurting both your reputation and your profits.

A powerful strategy we recently discovered is not only ranking well in Google searches but also running simple and inexpensive Google Ads. For example, when someone Googles "WebinarKit," we have ads running with keywords like "WebinarKit reviews," "WebinarKit testimonials," and "What are people saying about WebinarKit?" We run two straightforward ads: one directs to our homepage, and the other leads to an optimized testimonials page with over 300 reviews. The ad simply states, "WebinarKit reviews: What are people saying about WebinarKit?" This strategy has led to a significant increase in sales.

The pipeline works like this: when we run ads to WebinarKit and our webinars, people then Google us. So, we're creating Google searches by running Facebook ads. Wouldn't you want to capitalize on those Google searches by getting in front of the people there, too, versus letting it go to competitors? So essentially, we're the first thing that pops up on Google Ads. So now we have a pipeline where our Facebook ads create the initial awareness. The second step is for people to then Google us, and we are right there to capture those warm audiences for very, very cheap with Google Ads and search engine optimization. And then, you've created a really strong branding pipeline that can help you see even better results in your business.

Another concept that I've learned in business is what I like to call the love language of marketing. The concept of love languages is simply that people bond over different mediums. The traditional five love languages are physical touch, words of affirmation, acts of service, receiving gifts, and quality time. It's a different set of ways to "bond" with online content, but essentially the same concept. We've touched on this a bit earlier, but some people might not want to sit through an hour-and-a-half presentation. That's just simply true. These are just optimization tactics, so you don't necessarily need to start with them or even incorporate them midway. However, spreading your message across different mediums will ultimately lead to increased conversions. What if you turned your webinar into various formats?

When we talk about marketing love languages, we're referring to the different ways people resonate with messaging. For example, some individuals prefer a direct sales pitch with no time wasted, while others appreciate a more gradual approach, where they feel valued and special.

Let's explore different ways to appeal to these varied marketing preferences. First, let's discuss turning your webinar into different types of events. We covered this extensively in the previous chapter, but to summarize, multi-day events are a powerful way to move people through your content at a steady rate, keep them continuously engaged and focused on your message, help them connect more with your message and achieve those multiple touch points that we've been saying throughout this book are just so important. All those things are going to greatly boost your conversion and sales.

Now, along the same vein, you can do the same thing by taking your webinar content and converting it into a different type of event like a summit, course content, challenge, or something along those lines. This is another completely viable type of event that might resonate more with certain customers compared to others, especially when contrasted with a standard 90-minute-plus webinar. Thanks to the power of AI, converting your existing webinar presentation into a new format is easier than ever. Simply take the outline of your content and use an AI tool like ChatGPT or Cloud AI. Ask it to convert your webinar into a summit, course, or multi-day event, and the tool will break down the content accordingly. You'll be surprised at how effectively it can transform your webinar into the new format you requested. From there, you can tweak and modify the content to your liking. It's incredibly easy to repurpose your content this way. Once you've developed a standard webinar format, it's a breeze to convert it into another format that might better resonate with a different segment of your audience.

In addition to turning your webinar into various event types, you can also cater to different marketing love languages by creating articles and blog posts. Not everyone has the time or inclination to watch a long webinar, but they might be willing to read a quick article or blog post. By converting your webinar content into written form, you can reach segments of your audience who prefer to consume content at their own pace. This is a simple and effective way to leverage your existing content to appeal to a broader audience, especially those who favor reading over watching videos.

Now, another awesome benefit with this particular strategy is that by having these articles and blog posts on your website, you can build your SEO or search engine optimization so that you can start getting more organic traffic to your website and ultimately to your offer, your product, and getting more sales. Turning your webinar content or transcript into articles and blog posts can be as simple as dividing your content into sections, which can then be pasted directly into different blog posts or articles and slightly tweaked, such as by adding an introduction and a conclusion. It's a straightforward process. Alternatively, AI has made this even easier. You can paste your entire webinar transcript into an AI tool and ask it to convert the content into articles and blog posts. You'll be surprised at how effectively it handles the task.

Don't miss out on this easy opportunity to extend the reach of your existing webinar content. In addition to converting your content into different types of events, blog posts, and articles, you can also turn it into a short-form video sales letter (VSL). This is another quick win with your WebinarKit to reach yet another audience segment through a different marketing channel.

If you're unfamiliar with what a VSL is, it's essentially a short video that gives a concise overview of a product or service, often featured at the top of a company's website. You can easily create the same thing by converting your long-form webinar into a short-form VSL. With AI, this is simpler than ever—just paste your webinar content into an AI tool and ask it to distill the highlights into a short-form video script. In no time, you'll have a VSL script ready to use on your product page, social media, or even as a paid ad. From our personal experience, the results can be impressive.

Another great way to repurpose your webinar content is by converting it into a mini-webinar, which is similar to a VSL but slightly different. Sometimes, less is more for certain audiences. While some people prefer a longer 90-minute to 2-hour webinar, others may resonate better with a shorter video. That's why it's worth experimenting with this format once you have your main webinar set up, as outlined earlier in the book.

Converting your longer webinar into a shorter version or mini-webinar can be extremely useful and beneficial. It's a simple process: Just take your pre-recorded or live webinar and edit out the less crucial or "fluffier" parts, keeping only the most important content. This is an easy way to leverage your existing webinar material and create a new, concise webinar that can help you re-engage with your current audience and reach new audiences as well.

Lastly, another effective way to repurpose your webinar content and tap into different marketing love languages is by turning it into organic Instagram Reels, TikToks, YouTube Shorts, and other short-form videos on social media. Short-form video content is immensely popular these days—people are obsessed with TikToks, Instagram Reels, YouTube Shorts, and similar formats. These types of posts are all the rage and can go viral quickly.

You've likely seen examples yourself, so it's clear that turning your webinar content into these potentially viral TikToks, YouTube Shorts, Instagram Reels, etc., could be highly beneficial. This is easy to do since you already have your main webinar content. Whether you have a pre-recorded or live session, you can simply clip out key moments from your webinar and transform them into short-form videos to post on social media or use in paid advertising to reach new audiences.

Hopefully, you can see just how powerful and straightforward this can be. By selecting key moments that are particularly relevant or impactful, you can easily convert them into potentially viral, high-impact social media posts. With all these methods and examples of different marketing love languages, it's clear how easy it is to repurpose and leverage your webinar content in various powerful ways to connect with new audiences and customers.

Now that we've wrapped up the section on marketing love languages, let's talk about the power of retargeting or remarketing. If you're not familiar with these terms, don't worry—they're not as complicated as they might sound. Retargeting or remarketing refers to reaching out to, advertising to, or engaging with people who have previously interacted with you or your content. Throughout this book, we've discussed the importance of touchpoints—the more touchpoints you have with someone, the more likely they are to buy from you.

Think about the last time you purchased a big-ticket item. You probably didn't buy from the first brand you encountered. Instead, you might have seen an ad, done a Google search, or clicked on their product page. After that, you likely noticed more ads for that product or brand, keeping it in the back of your mind. Maybe you even went back to their website and signed up for a coupon, planning to make the purchase. But then, something distracted you—a text message, a phone call—and you closed the website without completing your order. But then they started sending you follow-up emails reminding you to complete your order, and you finally completed the purchase. This is just a quick general example of what retargeting can look like in practice. And the results can be massive.

Essentially, all they've been doing here is once they've had that initial touchpoint with you, they're just following up with you over and over until you eventually convert and become that customer. So again, don't be scared by the term retargeting or remarketing. It might sound a little advanced, but it's actually not a difficult concept at all. And you can definitely leverage this for yourself and your business. And frankly, it's something that we'd recommend to pretty much any individual or business that's selling things just because of how enormously powerful it can be. Now, you might think doing all of this sounds super complicated: *How do I do this? How am I gonna set this up? This sounds like I need to do some coding or something super technical.* The truth is, to get started with retargeting or remarketing, it's really not that difficult just to start doing this in your own business with your webinar funnels especially. And you can set up some basic remarketing automations in no time at all with the right webinar platform like WebinarKit, for example.

A Reminder to grab our free resources, which come with this book, for a fully in-depth explanation of setting up retargeting and remarketing.
Scan the QR code:

or go to https://getwebinarkit.com/book-resources

But here's just a quick example of how you can immediately get started with this in your own webinars in no time at all. Say you've set up your first webinar and webinar funnel, you're driving traffic to your registration page, you're starting to get people to watch your presentation, and you might already be starting to see your first sales trickle in. But it doesn't just end there. A quick way to immediately boost your results is to leverage remarketing/retargeting. To do it in the webinar context, simply send some follow-up emails to your attendees after the main event that they signed up for is over. In your follow-up emails, you could just direct them to your sales page so that they can go see your offer.

So, even if they didn't convert live during the webinar pitch, they can then check out your offer later on. An even more powerful approach (as discussed previously) is to direct them to a replay page with a countdown timer, explaining that your offer is discounted for a limited time until the timer expires. This can be an incredibly effective way of remarketing to those who have registered for your event, hitting multiple touchpoints, and following up with them consistently until they become customers.

So, don't be intimidated by the seemingly advanced term "remarketing" or "retargeting." All we're doing here is reaching out to people who have already engaged with us in the past—people who are more likely to be warm or hot leads, meaning they're more likely to be ready to purchase from you. This is a simple and easy strategy to implement in your first webinar, yet it's an immensely powerful way to start leveraging remarketing and achieving better results with your webinars and business right away.

Be sure to check out the free resources that come with this book for more examples of remarketing methods, as well as in-depth tutorials on setting everything up.

In addition to this, let's delve deeper into the power of building your audience and community. We briefly touched on this earlier, specifically the importance of directing people to a community on the thank-you page they see after signing up for your webinar. What's really powerful about this is that anyone who has been through your webinar and joined your community already understands your message the way you intend it to be understood. They've followed your "hero's journey," so to speak, and are familiar with your narrative.

This community is composed of people who already know, like, and trust you and who will continue interacting with each other. This interaction creates legitimacy for your brand because it shows that others share and understand your message—your audience isn't alone in following your vision. While an email list is valuable, it's a one-way communication tool. Regardless of the size of your list, recipients don't know if they're the only ones getting the email or if it's being sent to thousands. This doesn't necessarily boost your perceived status or influence. In contrast, a community allows people to see that you're not only an expert in your field with a successful webinar but also the leader of a thriving community built around your vision. This significantly enhances your legitimacy and credibility.

Community marketing has become increasingly important in recent years, especially as more people encounter bad offers and poor marketing practices. The need to build trust has grown exponentially, and this is where creating a community can truly set you apart. If you start building a genuine community, people will see you in an even higher regard than they would from just attending a webinar or being part of an email list. On your thank-you page and in your follow-up emails after the webinar, we highly recommend incorporating some form of community element. You'll thank us later for this advice.

Based on your webinar, we've discussed the importance of touchpoints and how to create various assets. By transforming your webinar content into different formats, you'll have an endless stream of material to keep promoting to your audience. Some people advocate sending daily emails to their newsletter, but the key is consistency. If you want to send daily emails, that would be great. If you prefer weekly emails, that's also a good place to start. At a minimum, we would say that you want to keep in touch with your newsletter at least once a week.

Conclusion

First off, I want to congratulate you—you made it to the end of the book. Most people buy books, let them sit on their shelves, and never even get close to finishing them. But you made it to the conclusion. You've absorbed information that could change your business and life in record time and reached the finish line. So, first of all, congratulations on making it this far.

The knowledge in this book can separate successful entrepreneurs from those who don't reach their sales goals. Now that you've made it to this point, I want to share a couple of final points. If you apply the concepts in this book to your business, you will be able to generate sales, period. That doesn't mean there won't be some tweaking involved, but we hope you see that in this day and age, it has never been easier to harness the power of one-to-many selling, automate that process, and use AI to build the entire system in record time. You no longer need to guess who your customer avatar is or what marketing messages will work best.

It's never been easier to start right out of the gate with messaging that turns a stranger into a buyer. And with webinars, as we've discussed, you can maximize both short-term, immediate buyers, and long-term buyers who join your audience. With that in mind, a couple of key points to remember: You definitely want to have a webinar in your business. Whether you run it live or automated isn't the first question you should be asking. The first question should be, "How quickly can I get my webinar up and running?"

If you've read this book, you know the answer: as soon as a couple of days from now. We highly recommend following the framework we've laid out for you, as it took us years to develop. Follow what we teach about AI, and you'll be well on your way to creating a business and life-changing webinar—it's never been easier. Additionally, guard this book carefully and apply its lessons as a secret weapon in your business again and again. As we've mentioned, what we teach here is something you can turn on and off whenever you need new clients. You can leave it running simultaneously or use it whenever you need an injection of new business or sales. Just like Trevor, who turns his webinar on and off whenever he needs new clients—the last time he did that, he generated 20 new high-ticket clients in record time. We use webinars in various ways in our business, both automated and live. Over time, as you apply webinars in your business, you'll see how easy it is to do the same.

With that, we want to leave you with a couple of final pieces of advice beyond webinars. Be careful about who you take advice from, and focus on surrounding yourself with people and narratives that support your goals and dreams. After reading this book, we want to say congratulations again and thank you. Here are the next steps we recommend:

Once you understand the power of the content in this book, we've made it easier for you to take those next steps.

What's possible now?

Once you've consumed this content, it's possible to transform your business completely. We've made this easy for you in a couple of ways.

Throughout this book, we've provided a powerful set of resources to help you apply what you've learned to the next level in record time.

Scan the QR code:

or go to https://getwebinarkit.com/book-resources

These tools and access to AI will help you build everything in record time. This is a totally new development—building your entire webinar ecosystem in just a couple of days has never been possible before. Previously, it would have taken months. Now is the time to act and take advantage of how quickly you can get started. We've made it easy for you to take these next steps.

Over the years, we've developed products and services that have worked to grow our business. So now that we've reinforced all the main points...

I want to take a quick second to talk about how the right platform can help you take all the knowledge you've gained from this book and put it into practice. You've got all the knowledge you need to get started, and if you've made it this far and want to turn that knowledge into action, the easiest way possible is through our platform, WebinarKit. WebinarKit has everything you need to get started with building and running your webinars in the shortest amount of time. You can be up and running in literally just minutes. At the time of writing this, over 18,000 businesses have interacted with the tool, with more trying it out and becoming full users every day.

WebinarKit allows you to apply every concept we've covered in this book, whether you want to run automated webinars, just-in-time webinars, instant watch webinars, live webinars, five-day challenges, multi-week series, or anything in between. WebinarKit has the features you need to do so easily.

All the various aspects that go into making a powerful, high-converting webinar funnel are readily available and easy to use on our platform. For example, you can get your high-converting registration and thank you pages, your webinar presentation or watch room, and your replay page set up in just minutes with our powerful drag-and-drop visual builders. You can host it on our platform, meaning you don't even need your own website to get started. If you do have a website and prefer to use it, you can easily embed our registration forms, thank you widgets, or even the watch room itself on any of your web pages. Plus, our latest AI features let you set up your content faster than ever.

With our engagement-boosting features like live chat, question boxes, visual offers, polls, handouts, and simulated chat messages, you'll have everything you need to keep your audience engaged during your presentation, maximizing conversions and sales. As we've outlined throughout this book, webinars can effectively tap into human psychology, and WebinarKit helps you leverage those insights for the best possible results. You can also use our built-in email and text messaging features to maximize attendee show-up rates, send follow-up messages to boost conversions and leverage our powerful segmentation features to send specific messages to specific groups in your audience, such as reminders to anyone who didn't attend your webinar. Alternatively, you can use our powerful native integrations to connect with popular CRM and email service provider platforms.

WebinarKit also offers multi-language support, allowing you to customize the user interface and labels that registrants and attendees see as they move through your webinar funnel. This makes webinars a powerful tool for reaching a global audience.

Last but not least, with WebinarKit's white-label features, you can even resell sub-accounts under your own brand name, essentially turning WebinarKit into your software. That means not only can you use WebinarKit to generate revenue and profit by running your own webinars, but your customers and clients can also benefit from the power of webinars in their businesses.

As you can see, the right platform will let you take all the concepts and strategies we've covered in this book and put them into practice. Whether you want to try out WebinarKit or not, we hope that by reading this book, you've seen how powerful webinars can be for your business and how attainable they are for anyone who wants to get started. And just as a reminder, whether or not you're interested in WebinarKit, you will always have access to the completely free gifts and resources included in this book.

These free resources can supercharge your webinar results and provide a deeper dive into all the concepts and strategies we've covered in this book. So be sure to check them out.

We hope you've come away from this with a clear understanding of the full power of webinars and feel empowered to build and run one for yourself. Whether it's for your own business and financial success or to achieve your deeper underlying "why"—whether that's leaving your nine-to-five job to travel the world or gaining the financial independence you've always wanted—webinars can help you get there. We hope you'll take the concepts and strategies from this book and put them into action.

Take the next step in your journey by grabbing our free resources here:

Scan the QR code:

Or, use this link to grab our resources here:
https://getwebinarkit.com/book-resources

Check out WebinarKit for automated webinars and events here:
https://getwebinarkit.com/

Check out WebinarKit Live for live webinars here:
https://getwebinarkit.com/live

Check out WebinarKit White Label to turn WebinarKit into your own branded software here:
https://getwebinarkit.com/white-label

THANK YOU FOR READING OUR BOOK!

DOWNLOAD YOUR FREE GIFTS

Just to say thanks for buying and reading our book, we would like to give you a few free bonus gifts, no strings attached!

To Download Now, Visit:

or go to https://getwebinarkit.com/book-resources

We appreciate your interest in our book and value your feedback as it helps us improve future versions of this book. We would appreciate it if you could leave your invaluable review on Amazon.com with your feedback. Thank you!